STINKY THINKIN

STINKY THINKIN

My Story of Compulsive Gambling and Recovery

Albert L. Fisher, Jr.

First Printing 2022
ISBN: 979-8-9856542-9-5

Cover Design: Alex Wierda
Author Photos: Rachel Loren Photography

DEDICATIONS

This book is dedicated to my parents, Al and Rita; my grandmother, Elena; my children Al, Nikki, and Chris; my ex-wife Lisa and my wife Julie. I also dedicate this book to my grandchildren and future great grandchildren, so that they may understand the importance of making good decisions and how their lives can be positively impacted by them, or negatively impacted if they choose to make bad decisions. Good decisions make for a better life. It took me forty-eight years of my life to accept that. This book is also dedicated to every GA member with whom I have sat across a table from over more than the ten years. Thanks to each of you for helping me to change my life. I will never forget you. Finally, none of this would have been possible without my renewed faith in God. I can never praise Him enough for what He has taught me over the past ten and a half years. May God heal all those who suffer with an addiction, along with the loved ones of all addicts. Amen.

TABLE OF CONTENTS

DEDICATIONS ____________

ACKNOWLEDGEMENT ____________

CHAPTER 1 ____________ **1**

WHY A BOOK ON COMPULSIVE GAMBLING? ____________ 1

CHAPTER 2 ____________ **5**

MY FOUR DECADES OF COMPULSIVE GAMBLING ____________ 5

CHAPTER 3 ____________ **22**

THE LOSS OF PURPOSE ____________ 22

CHAPTER 4 ____________ **31**

WHAT GAMBLING COST ME ____________ 31

CHAPTER 5 ____________ **37**

MY EARLY YEARS OF RECOVERY ____________ 37

Recovery Year One - The Year of Fear ____________ 37

Recovery Year Two - The Year of Ben ____________ 40

Recovery Year Three – The Year of Julie ____________ 43

Recovery Year Four - The Year of Prostate Cancer and My Own Mortality ____________ 50

CHAPTER 6 ____________ **57**

THE POWER OF MUSIC IN MY RECOVERY ____________ 57

CHAPTER 7 ____________ **65**

JUMPING OFF THE CRAZY TRAIN ____________ 65

CHAPTER 8 ____________ **70**

PRISON, INSANITY OR DEATH ____________ 70

CHAPTER 9 ____________ **74**

GAMBLERS ANONYMOUS ____________ 74

CHAPTER 10 ______ 82

THE IMPORTANCE OF STEP ONE OF THE TWELVE STEPS ______ 82

CHAPTER 11 ______ 87

THE NECESSITY OF STEPS TWO & THREE OF THE TWELVE STEPS ______ 87

CHAPTER 12 ______ 97

WORKING STEPS FOUR THROUGH TWELVE ______ 97

CHAPTER 13 ______ 107

AL'S EIGHT STEPS TOWARD ACHIEVING A NEW LIFE AND MAINTAINING MY SOBRIETY ______ 107

Al's Step One – Go to Gamblers Anonymous ______ 108

Al's Step Two – Slow Down and Jump Off the Crazy Train ______ 110

Al's Step Three - Forgive Yourself and Quit Chasing Your Losses ______ 111

Al's Step Four – Come to Terms with Your Shoulders ______ 113

Al's Step Five – The Strength of Family ______ 114

Al's Step Six – A Good Woman ______ 115

Al's Step Seven – Staying Positive ______ 116

Al's Step Eight – Never Forget ______ 118

CHAPTER 14 ______ 120

OLD AL COMPARED TO NEW AL (MY TWO LIVES) 120

CHAPTER 15 ______ 135

FOR LOVED ONES OF THE COMPULSIVE GAMBLER OR ADDICT ______ 135

CHAPTER 16 ______ 138

CONCLUSION ______ 138

ACKNOWLEDGEMENTS

This book poured out of me after four years of sobriety. Without the support of my family, both by blood and GA, this book would never exist. I wish to thank all the members of GA with whom I have sat across from as we struggled to manage the demon within us to better our lives. Special thanks to Jim A., Mike B., Ernie O., and Carol B. for guiding me through my early years of recovery.

CHAPTER 1

WHY A BOOK ON COMPULSIVE GAMBLING?

That's a good question. First, I am writing it for me and my loved ones, so all may better understand the disease within me. Second, if I can help anyone with an addiction to recognize that they can overcome their disease, that would make some sense out of the life I previously led. I know like no one else can, other than another addict, how difficult it is to break from your addiction. As a compulsive gambler I know how badly I wanted to quit, yet my disease would not allow it as I would do nothing different to assist in making that happen. Mainly, I believe telling my story may give hope to serious problem gamblers and any others who have lived a life in the throes of addiction; that upon reading my story they might realize if I could quit gambling after forty-eight years of active gambling, they may learn they could do it as well.

As for the title of my book, Stinky Thinkin? This relates to the frame of mind addicts and nonaddicts alike indulge in, leading us to make bad decisions and making our lives worse. Stinky thinking takes over and clouds an addicted person's sense of reality. In the depths of my addiction, I truly believed that my compulsive gambling was best for me and my family, believing the "big win" would solve all our issues.

I'm convinced that compulsive gambling is a disease in my brain. Addiction is baffling as it makes you believe what you know to be wrong as being right. I gambled over four decades with this illusion, thinking I was perfectly fine doing it. As a compulsive gambler, I was a chronic liar. Today I often speak at Gambler's Anonymous (GA) about how I would lie when it was totally unnecessary for me to do so. That is one of the behavioral characteristics that changes with addiction. You lie. You lie even when it serves no purpose.

Another consequence of addiction is that you hurt yourself, as well as any loved one or acquaintance who may care about you in any way. My disease would use the people I love seemingly without consequence, all so I could dip further into the disease. To some degree I knew I was hurting myself as well as my loved ones. My addiction would take over and convince me that I was a bad person, and the only way to make things right to my loved ones and acquaintances was to win back the money I had lost. I gambled for decades chasing this vicious lie. You do so with little to no concern or even realization of what or why you're even doing it.

There's no doubt in my mind that there are millions of serious problem gamblers today who do not consider themselves compulsive gamblers. The disease plays with your mind. It's as though you have an angel on one shoulder speaking internally to you and the devil on the other shoulder speaking as well. So, you have these two competing forces, good versus evil, fighting for control of your mind and actions. What I've learned is that as a compulsive gambler, the devil controls ninety percent of my mind and actions while my internal angel controls only ten percent. This is how despicable this disease is for a compulsive gambler. I knew deep down that what I was thinking and doing was wrong, or a series of bad choices. The ninety percent, however, controlled my life and actions, meaning that when my focus was to gamble, which it was over ninety percent of my time, the ten percent would only come out on the ride home or when I lost all my money for that evening. Then my disease would subside, and clarity would ensue, even though it was short-lived until I awakened the next morning. My focus the following morning would be to go right back, balls to the wall to obtain the money necessary to recoup my losses, with no thought of potentially increasing my losses and so on and on.

Another reason I'm writing my story of addiction is because of Gamblers Anonymous (GA). First off, GA and its members helped to save my life, so I have nothing but respect for the program, and especially the people I have met within it. The sad thing is as a compulsive gambler, you have no other options for recovery. You can go to a doctor, and they will refer you to a psychologist. This happened with me when my doctor of ten years ran out of the room when I told him I needed help because of being a compulsive gambler. He walked out in disgust and five minutes later a nurse came in with an authorization to see a psychologist. That was the last time I saw my doctor of ten years. Then I proceeded to go once a week for three or four sessions to see the psychologist, and then I stopped when I learned there is no magic pill to rid me of this disease. I wanted something fast and painless. I believe what GA teaches you is that there is nothing fast in ridding yourself of this disease. It's one day at a time for life. Some in the program would challenge that, saying it's one day at a time but for me I believe it is for life and that I need to look at it that way. That thought process would not be good for someone new to the program because they must scratch, claw, and do whatever is necessary for that given day. Focusing beyond today for them would be detrimental because they have enough to worry about today and not to gamble.

Over the past fifty years, availability to gambling has changed significantly. Every gas station you go into has state and federally sponsored lottery tickets and numbers, Keno in dining establishments, off track betting parlors providing betting on horse races nationally and even internationally. Casinos once relegated solely to Las Vegas and then Atlantic City, are now located throughout the country as well as internationally. The reality is that people who never had an issue with gambling are now becoming compulsive gamblers due to ease of access and other realities in their lives. Gambling today is both state and federally sponsored to assist our government and lawmakers with increased taxes and various financial perks, all at the expense of the one to two percent of us who become compulsive gamblers and are anonymous. Sounds like a win-win for the government and the casino operators and a lose-lose for the compulsive gambler and their loved ones as they are just as affected.

There is also that stigma that a compulsive gambler is a degenerate individual who is self-centered and only cares about themselves. I am telling you that is absolutely untrue. I have met some of the finest individuals within the GA community. Those that can achieve sobriety for a lengthy period of time find that the ninety percent of the devil's influence and the ten percent of the angel's influence that I speak of earlier in this chapter experience a complete reversal of this reality in their lives. This means that over ninety percent of my life and actions are now controlled by the angel on my one shoulder, instead of the devil on my other shoulder that has been reduced to less than ten percent, in my thought process. I think that since legalized gambling has changed so dramatically over the past twenty years, GA must change as well because we are not touching all those suffering that I believe we can and should be touching.

CHAPTER 2

MY FOUR DECADES OF COMPULSIVE GAMBLING

I was gambling as early as I can remember so I say at age four. My mom and dad were both loving, hardworking parents who were both compulsive gamblers. My dad loved the horses, and my mom loved the slot machines. Some of my favorite memories were taking off of school, meeting up with my dad at 35 Street South Halsted corner restaurant to eat and read that day's horse racing program to begin picking winners before we ever reached the racetrack. We used to have newspaper and magazine stands and right across the street from the restaurant was a stand that offered the Daily Racing Form and each racetrack's program for the day. Generally, there would be thoroughbreds during the daytime and harness racing at night. We thought it was a great day if we could last through the thoroughbred races and then head out to the harness racetrack in the evening to gamble some more. By saying if we could last, I'm speaking that if we still had money available after the first racetrack. Very rarely did we complete a doubleheader by going to both tracks in one day.

I grew up in Chicago on the south side near old Mayor Daley's Bridgeport Neighborhood, so we would frequent Hawthorne Racecourse and Sportsman's Park more frequently since they were also on the south side, rather than Maywood Park and Arlington Park which were further away. We enjoyed both thoroughbred and harness racing. I can remember going to both Hawthorne and Sportsman's Park on a Friday night to bet on Rambling Willie who was our favorite racehorse. Bob Farrington was his driver, and he was my and my dad's favorite driver. Some of my best memories as a kid was watching Rambling Willie win and my dad and I being so happy together.

I will always remember the time I spent my entire summer break in New York City by my aunt, uncle, and cousins. They lived on Bleecker Street which I believe was in Queens. This is where I learned those three infamous letters and carry them with me even to this day. The letters were OTB, and they stood for off track betting, and this was the first time I had ever seen or heard of such a thing. At this OTB I could get people to bet for me on horses that ran in the New York State area. What a great time and place for a kid around ten years old who was also a compulsive gambler. My aunt and uncle took me and my cousins from Chicago to Rock City USA/Ruby Falls/Incline Railroad just outside Chattanooga, Tennessee. I would highly recommend visiting them as I still remember them fondly to this day. Then we went to North Carolina and back to New York for the rest of my summer break from school until a week before Labor Day when my parents would come to New York to pick me up and take me back home to Chicago. My cousin Eddie was a little older than me and was just as crazy a gambler as I was. I can remember walking with him to Myrtle Avenue OTB to figure out who we could find that would place our bets for us. We never had a problem finding someone to bet for us. We would even go inside the OTB to recruit someone until we were shooed away by their security.

Those were the days. We would get our bets in and next door to the OTB was a Carvel ice cream store. Even better, my cousin John's girlfriend Cathy was the manager at the store. Cathy was awesome. Carvel was awesome. They had the best chocolate ice cream cone with chocolate sprinkles I have ever tasted to this day. I always would think that my cousin John better marry her, or I would when I got older. Cathy was always good to me. I can't thank her enough for her kindness, but that's just the type of person she was.

I truly enjoyed that summer even though I really did miss my parents. When my Uncle John came home from work, we would either head out to the Atlantic Ocean on the boat he owned and go fishing, or we would be off to Yonkers multiple times a week. I couldn't wait for Uncle John to come home. He was a great man. I miss him. My Aunt Toni was a fireball. I've never met someone so loving as her and almost at the same time, so scary. She did not mince words. You always knew what was on her mind, even when you didn't want to know. My cousin Rita was the one I felt closest to. I loved her accent, a very thick, strong, New York accent. It was great and so was she. She rarely gambled with me, except for playing poker, but I used to get a kick out of her on her CB all night saying "Breaker 1-9" to the truckers and conversing with them. Little did they know Rita was around my age. They would also stay up late and around 2 a.m. to 3 a.m., send Eddie or John to the bakery to get freshly made French bread and was it fresh. The bread would still be warm to hot by the time one of them would get back to the house with it. Just great memories from that summer and gambling played a significant part in all of that. Therefore, it is difficult for me to hate gambling, but I do. I hate what it did to me and how it controlled me and negatively affected my life for the bulk of it, and I hate how it affects so many others like me and attempts to destroy their futures.

On Saturday nights I learned how to play poker, watching my dad and my uncles play. I used this knowledge occasionally during my later years of grammar school, but predominantly throughout my high school years. A frequent hangout to gamble and eat donuts was Winchell's Donut Shop, next to Kelly High School. I remember one day after school a group of us students met up at Winchell's and proceeded to play poker for the next three hours. Now back in the day there were no cell phones, texting, or emails, so when I arrived home around 8 p.m., over four hours late from when I should have been home, my mother, who had a hot Lithuanian temper, was ready to spank me like I hadn't been spanked in years. As I walked in, she asked me where I was and what had I been doing, as she got up to begin beating me. I reached into my pants and pulled out over one-hundred-dollar bills that I had won playing poker at Winchell's. As soon as she saw the money, she immediately hugged me, smiling, and asking me how much I was going to give her. Then I asked her how much I would have to give her to keep from being beaten by her. She said half of the money. So, I gave her half the money, and all was right again with the world. I think there was a learning somewhere within that episode, but I'll leave it to others to figure out.

I can remember during my sophomore year in high school, being one of two school bookies for the Super Bowl and having a one-thousand-dollar side bet on the Pittsburgh Steelers straight up versus the Dallas Cowboys. I was a big Terry Bradshaw, Lynn Swann, and Steel Curtain fan. When Pittsburgh won, I was on cloud nine. I still remember that feeling of being paid the one-thousand dollars from my competition that Monday. I give him credit. He paid me one-thousand dollars in cash. As I was hovering over cloud nine, I never considered what effect the loss had on the person I had just won from or how I would have handled losing if I had lost. That is so typical for a compulsive gambler. No matter how many times you lose, when your mind is in action and you're getting ready to bet, you are thoroughly consumed with winning. Losing never enters the equation until the unthinkable actually happens and you lose. What a crazy disease. How do you not consider the possibility that you may lose? I truly do not know because I never considered that I would lose, at least not until the last five to ten years of my gambling. At that point, especially the last five years, I knew I was going to lose; yet I still could not stop gambling even though I truly felt that way.

I can remember betting on a turf race at Hawthorne and I bet two dollars to win on a fifty to one shot. My dad bet twenty dollars to win on the favorite at odds of two to one. The race goes off and my horse beats my dad's horse by a nose and pays over one-hundred dollars to win. Another big win of mine in high school was when I played two dollars to win, place and show on Chief Timmy Hawk. It was either at Sportsman's Park or Hawthorne. He was fifteen to one in the paper. In order to make the race I had to leave school two periods early that day and take multiple Chicago Transit Authority (CTA) buses to the racetrack to bet on Chief Timmy Hawk. When I made it to the track, his odds were now forty-five to one. Even though his odds were higher I put two dollars to win, place and show on him. He ended up winning that race at odds of fifty to one, and I collected over one-hundred seventy dollars from my six-dollar bet. Then my biggest concern was making it back home safely with all the money I had won. I never thought about getting home until the race was over.

I remember another gambling event at Maywood Park Racetrack with my best friend, Ron. Ron was not a compulsive gambler. He could place two dollars to win on a horse, while I had two hundred dollars on another horse. One time he had two dollars on a six to one shot, and I had two hundred dollars to win on a two to one shot. Both he and I are outside by the fence and finish line screaming for our horses to win. His horse beats mine by a nose. He is so happy. I am so sick. I believe I told him after I would have given him twenty dollars if mine had won, like his rooting for his horse placed the whammy on mine. Oh, the mind of a compulsive gambler.

As a compulsive gambler these are the events you remember. These memories are what kept me gambling for over four decades of my life. As a compulsive gambler, somehow you remember your wins and you forget your losses. Since I have lost many more times than I have won, you would think that I would remember losing much more than winning. For a compulsive gambler, all you remember are the wins. That is until you lose it all one night, and when you are out of money and with no ability to get additional money, then reality comes raging back. You realize all of those losses. You realize the repetition of losses over and over again. You vow to yourself and any loved one who will listen that you have learned gambling does not pay and that you must stop. It's amazing how many times that after losing all my money, then heading home down the highway, how many times I would search for the right tree to crash into and end my addiction. As I found the correct tree, I then would realize that somehow, I would mess things up by running into it and paralyze myself where someone would have to care for me the rest of my life.

I have had other gambling highlights throughout my years. Compulsive gambling is a progressive disease and my gambling progressed to unthinkable proportions. I will say, I never considered my gambling to be compulsive or a disease of any kind during my first forty years of gambling. When I went to GA the first time, I never considered my gambling as a disease. I was simply weak.

When I was a kid, I could bet two dollars on a horse and be happy. In my teens I had to bet at least twenty dollars plus on a horse. Once married and with children and nearing my thirties, I would need to bet two hundred dollars plus on a horse or two hundred dollars on a roulette wheel picking numbers. By the time I hit my forties and my mid-life crisis ensued, things really began to ratchet up. I was married for twenty-one years. They were difficult years. I loved my wife and I believe she loved me, but my compulsive gambling coupled with her marrying me so young and not dating enough prior to marrying severely impacted our relationship. She was sixteen and I was nineteen when we were married. It was never my plan to get married that early in my life or to marry someone so young, but I fell in love, and I fell hard. If I could have changed anything, it would have been my gambling. My ex-wife knew I was a gambler. A definite giveaway was when we were dating, I would stop at the Off-Track Betting facility with her in the car. I would run in and make my bets for the day and then we would be off to do whatever else we had planned for the day. Being married to a compulsive gambler is not something I would recommend. Running away prior to marrying a compulsive gambler is something I would recommend. My ex-wife tried to help me with my gambling problem. I always think it ridiculous when I hear commercials tell you where to call if you think you have a gambling problem. Compulsive gambling is so beyond a problem, not even close to simply being a problem. So many times, I wanted to stop but couldn't.

After fifteen years of my marriage, my wife had enough for the second or third time and ordered me to GA or that she would divorce me and take the kids. The last thing I wanted was to lose my family. I would do anything to keep that from happening, or so I thought. So, I began going to the Saturday night GA meeting in Libertyville, Illinois. I did this for over twelve months. I stayed clean for that period. My wife and I decided that we would celebrate with a two-week Hawaiian vacation for the family once I achieved one year of clean time. I worked the program or at least thought I was. I took on a sponsor. I worked the twelve steps with my sponsor or at least attempted to. In reality I did not complete any of the steps, even though we worked through steps one through six. During that twelve- and one-half-month period my life had improved immeasurably. I was paying off debt, not making new debt and saving money. As difficult a time as that period was for me personally, it was also some of the best times for my family and me. I achieved one year of clean time and was ready to receive my one-year coin and then to go on my trip to Hawaii. I learned the week before our trip that my one-year celebration was being postponed until I came back as another member's one-year clean date was coming up and they would combine our celebrations together. That didn't work for me. Stinky thinking came into play. I questioned in my mind why my celebration had to be pushed back and it affected me. My disease tripped me up with anger and some resentment on receiving my one-year coin closer to thirteen months rather than twelve months of clean time. We went on our family vacation and had an outstanding time.

When we made it back to Chicago, I was excited to attend the next GA meeting to receive my pin and give several influential members some gifts that I picked up for them from the island. That Saturday comes and goes without me attending. I can't remember my excuse for not attending but I did not. The following Saturday I also missed. The third Saturday I decided to attend. As I was on my way to GA, stinky thinking took over and I ended up at the Waukegan Off Track Betting facility and I was back active into my addiction again. This time I was going to do things differently and control my gambling. I was not going to allow it to control me. Mind you, these are the same words I would use each time that I tried to stop and then started gambling again. What a crock of crap. That is stinky thinking at its finest or at its worst, I guess. For a couple of weeks, I believed I was in control. I was betting up to only a certain amount. I was not staying and betting every race all night long. I picked my winners and layed off everything else. It took me about a month or two to realize that I was back to an uncontrollable life of gambling with no hope in sight, once again jeopardizing my marriage and my family.

One thing I want to make very clear is that nothing was more important to me than my wife and my children, absolutely nothing. Yet three to four years later, I was divorced after being married for twenty-one years. I was filing for bankruptcy and my 401k of over two hundred thousand dollars was down to zero. At this point I was at the lowest point in my life. Many would call that hitting rock bottom, but what I've learned about rock bottom is that if you continue to gamble, you will continue to achieve an even greater bottom each and every time. So, the only way to hit rock bottom is to stop gambling. Whatever bottom that is, that will be your lowest point if you stop gambling. Any compulsive gambler can tell you that when you think you're at your lowest point, all you must do is continue to gamble to reach an even lower point. An analogy I use in GA is that gambling is as if you're digging your own grave. You're standing six feet deep in it and yet you continue to go down deeper with the shovel, and eventually you recognize the dirt you are attempting to toss out is simply going up in the air and coming back down squarely upon your head. Every time a compulsive gambler gambles, you can rest assured a new bottom will be created. Unless you have lived it, it's hard to imagine how lonely and scary hitting bottom really is or hoping that is actually the bottom with no further descent. So that was my bottom. I can remember my ex-wife telling me that she did not want to be around when I eventually hit my rock bottom. I didn't like her saying that but when I think about it, I don't blame her. It was what I expected and hoped was my final bottom.

I've already stated compulsive gambling is a progressive disease. After my divorce, those next seven years for me were very dark. I lost my wife and family. I lost my home. I lost my job that I had worked for twenty-three years. I wasn't fired, I was downsized. I could have taken another position, but my ego had other ideas. I would move on to another company, better myself and never look back. To achieve this, I decided I needed a change of scenery and some distance, so I moved to the Grand Rapids area. I went from earning over one hundred thousand annually in a high leadership role, down to sixty percent of that with a less professional, more challenging organization. A key learning for a compulsive gambler is to appreciate what you have. I rarely did that, as I was always striving to accomplish more. It's so important to recognize and appreciate all that you have in this life, no matter how little you think that may be.

My oldest son began college around this time, and I was absolutely no use to him or to my daughter who was going to college in two years. As a compulsive gambler when you are firmly entrenched in the disease, the level of damage you incur upon your loved ones is unimaginable and unthinkable. Never in my wildest dreams did I think there would be a time in my life that I would not be there for my children. That simply was unconscionable for me. I believed I was put on this earth solely to develop three wonderful, loving, decent and good human beings in this world. It's as though life is filled with good and bad, as well as good and bad people. It was important for me to add to the numbers of good people in this world, as I believe good must overcome bad. My gambling negatively impacted my mom, dad, wife, children, aunts, uncles, cousins, friends, co-workers, and anyone else who came into contact with me and who cared for me. I was incapable of recognizing all the destruction that I caused due to my disease and how painful it was. This feeling of inflicting hurt upon loved ones kept me gambling for decades to try and make up for it. Regular gamblers will not understand how I can think in such a way, but a compulsive gambler will understand me and my plight in its entirety.

I can remember my son asking me what I thought about him giving plasma to earn money that he really needed, and I tried to talk him out of it. Yet in 2011 and 2012, I was providing plasma twice weekly in order to live. If I hadn't gambled, he would not have struggled as much as he did. He loaned me an ungodly amount of money to try and help me out, over twenty thousand dollars worth. He worked all summer painting houses and running his business to provide me money to live and with which to gamble. He finally learned that there was nothing he could do to get me to stop gambling and that he would no longer enable me and my gambling. I can remember my daughter needing to have an operation to clean out an infection that had affected a portion of her leg in college. I couldn't be there for her when I should have been. I did not have the money because I would gamble it all away. What a hopeless time for me as well as them.

By the end of my final seven years of gambling, I became an embezzler and a convicted felon due to my gambling. On March 4, 2011, I attended my first GA meeting in Grand Rapids. I was in a new, terrible bottom in my life. I was looking at potential prison time. I owed over twenty-two thousand dollars. I had no money and no way to pay it back. On Monday, March 7, I attended my second GA meeting in Grand Rapids. This meeting was led by a man with eleven years of clean time. That impressed me as I'd never met a GA member with that much clean time. At the meeting he spoke to me and the group that continuing to gamble would result in prison, insanity, or death. Those four words — prison, insanity, or death — continue to impact me to this day. I truly thought he was speaking directly to me. I was wondering how he knew that I might be heading to prison. That I was insane. Who could do all the stupid, negative things that I have done to myself and not be insane? Then finally death - how did he know that I had taken a large kitchen knife with me into the bathroom while I took a bath and imagined myself slicing both of my wrists, a practice I continued for two more weeks. How did he know that I wanted to die? Sadly, that is where this disease takes you. I believe that is its end game.

During my first year of recovery, the court placed me on five years of probation with twenty-four thousand dollars to be paid in restitution and court fees, and one-hundred and twenty hours of community service to be performed. At my sentencing hearing it was relayed that the one-hundred and twenty hours of community service were to be at the recycling plant. It seemed my prior employer was more concerned with me being sent to prison, even more so than the paying back of restitution money. This was primarily because they enjoyed telling new and potential associates how they have sent to prison previous associates who stole from them. Now when you hear them tell you that story, never in my wildest dreams did I ever think that I would become one of those people they are telling everybody about. Thankfully, the judge, the prosecutor and my lawyer were more focused on my paying back what I stole, and since I was working and beginning to make payments towards my restitution, they supported for me to stay out of the prison system.

My former employer should have been pleased with the recycling community service, as I would not wish that upon my worst enemy. I will never forget that experience. At my sentencing I was given six months to complete the one hundred twenty hours of community service, or so I thought. I went to the City of Wyoming where I was instructed that I had just under six weeks to complete it. The woman who ran the program was connected because when I told her that the judge gave me six months at sentencing to complete the hours, she told me, "Yeah, that's not my program. I know the judge said what he said, but this is the way my program works, and the amount of time provided for completion." I explained I was working at Walmart on overnights working over forty hours per week, and how then could I knock out the one hundred twenty thousand hours in less than six weeks? She told me that was not her problem, and she was right. It was not her problem; it was squarely mine.

After working 10 p.m. to 7 a.m. five nights a week, my youngest son would drop me off before 8 a.m. and pick me up from the recycling plant at 4 p.m. For the next five weeks, I worked three days a week at the recycling center and five nights a week at Walmart. Now I don't know if you have ever worked at a recycling plant, but here's what I can tell you. You are placed at one of two assembly lines with approximately twenty people on each line. The line moves and paper, cans, plastic and styrofoam move along as twenty pairs of hands are separating the items that are coming down the line. I would be remiss if I didn't mention the smell. You wore a paper mask over your face, but the odor is so foul my first day I gagged constantly and only an hour into the job I threw up. One thing that struck me that no one even thinks about is the fact that the City of Grand Rapids must find those forty pairs of hands needed to fill both lines daily. I'm sure people are placed throughout the country into a similar program as executed by the woman in the City of Wyoming, sending problem people in to do a job for which the city would otherwise pay. What a system; only in America! Thankfully, I lasted those five weeks while keeping my real job at Walmart. I will never forget that experience. It made me feel for all those people who are sent there that many in the community don't even know about.

With everything I went through, it was not the probation, court proceedings, restitution or community service that stopped my gambling. It was embarrassment, humility, pride, GA and certain select individuals who attended GA meetings during the early part of my recovery that assisted me in buying into the "One Day at A Time" program, and instead of worrying about speeding everything up, welcoming the slowness of recovery and not gambling each day as your recovery continues. It's a very peaceful place that, frankly, I never experienced when I was gambling. I appreciated the break from crazy thinking followed by crazy actions that used to be my life.

At my one-year anniversary of stopping gambling, I told the group that I have won over one million dollars on gambling in my lifetime but, unfortunately, I have lost over two million dollars. Then I said, "You can do the math from there." It sounded great initially, but in this case, reality does bite, and everyone in attendance knew what I was talking about. At that meeting one of our GA members mentioned that I was his hero as he would watch me when we were both at the same OTB facility. He talked about how he would watch me bet and collect, that he would get behind me in line to see what I was betting so he could bet the same. Never once did we speak at the OTB facility, and more revealing about where I was in all of this is that I did not even remember ever seeing him at the OTB facility. I was so into what I was going to do and all my problems, I noticed very little around me and my effect on others. So is the life of a compulsive gambler. I feel I must talk about this more. Jim A., who used the term prison, insanity, or death at my second GA meeting was right on for what a compulsive gambler and, in my opinion, any addict must look forward to as their disease progresses. What a terrible outcome for such a progressive disease.

Compulsive gamblers do not need to be in prison. I don't believe prison will take away the disease of compulsive gambling. To me this is only done to punish, like punishing a person with a disease is going to remove that disease from the individual. It's ludicrous and a financial waste for all states doing so. As overburdened as our judicial and prison systems are today, I believe the process is total bullshit. You would never see a person with cancer being put in prison simply because they have the disease. With saying that, I do believe in restitution. Repaying is crucial to our recovery. Where is the treatment? States and casinos make a lot of money from problem and normal gamblers, yet where is the treatment for those adversely affected who become ladened with this disease for the rest of their lives? The answer is nowhere, except for those we put in prison and that is not treatment, other than possibly inhumane treatment.

Michigan has a toll-free number for problem gamblers to call as I'm sure do many other states that allow legalized gambling within their state. That call gets sent to a recovered problem gambler who takes it. Most calls come from the spouse of the compulsive gambler with the consistent question, "What do I do?" Unfortunately, for the loved one of a compulsive gambler, there is actually very little you can do, other than to try and get your loved one's attention by leaving them or kicking them out, either forever or until they take their disease seriously and make GA a steady part of their life moving forward. I would love to see Big Pharma be compelled to work on treatment or possibly a cure for addictions of all kinds, to do the research and testing to make refraining from gambling as easy as taking a daily vitamin. I know it's not available now, but I believe it should be and some day could be.

What about having treatment facilities sponsored by the states and gambling companies throughout the United States to offer treatment for those afflicted, rather than sending them to prison or leaving them homeless on the streets or committing crimes to support their addiction until they are arrested. Prisons could reduce their populations with these treatment centers rising to treat the person's actual mental illness. This would also reduce the stress on our officers who every day make split decisions when arresting these nonviolent individuals after which these officers' actions are questioned. Sometimes they are sued because Monday morning quarterbacks have all the answers as to what they would do in a potentially life altering situation. I'm not claiming to be all knowing. I just believe the current system of sending diseased thinking, addicted people to prison simply keeps the reality of addiction at a lower volume within this country rather than the high level of noise that should be blasting throughout because of it. Not only with addicted people but including all family members negatively affected through addiction. The numbers of people involved would be ridiculous. The insanity of the disease is why I recommend these solutions.

When I gambled, I never thought of myself as insane. In fact, far from it. I thought I was it; very slick, able to juggle much more than the average person. Now I view myself as having been insane when I was active in my disease, without a doubt. My behavior and thinking were so far off from what I really think and who I really am. Thinking of myself as having been insane does not bother me. I believe it to be a fair representation of how I was at that time. I recognize that I'm only this way when I gamble and when I don't gamble, I'm nothing like it. Not even close. I believe this to be true with most addictions.

To me worst on the list of potential outcomes from gambling is death. There is no comeback from death. When I say death, I'm talking about suicide. That's another number you don't hear much about. I believe that's due to the massive number it would be and how shocked people would be with the sheer number of those who commit suicide due to their addiction and mental illness. All I know is that I never believed that I would ever contemplate suicide. Never ever. I was adamant about that. However, back in March 2011, I was suicidal for a two-week period of time, until I worked it out in my mind that I would be further harming my children, that I would be taking the easy way out for me, and the really hard thing to do would be to live my life one day at a time without gambling each day. I truly viewed recovery as my penance, to not be gambling and having to live the slowness of that type of life was my fitting prison for what I had done.

During the two-week period that I was suicidal, my thoughts were consumed that I would be doing my family a favor by killing myself. No longer would they have to live my ups and downs, mainly downs, when I gambled. My disease was really working on me to kill myself. I came to believe that was my disease's end game. What it wanted for me. I thank God for reaching me even when I didn't know it was Him, making me realize the lasting harm I would have done to my loved ones if I had taken my life. Every time I think back to those two weeks, I can't help but tear up as I remember that feeling of loneliness and hopelessness, coupled with helplessness. Thankfully, with God's help I made it out from that, but I can't help but feel for those where their addiction won, resulting in their taking their own life. Maybe it's not insanity. Simply by stopping gambling, stopping my addiction I no longer feel insane in any way. So, the learning, I believe, is that the disease causes the insanity, and when in recovery the insanity dissipates or is removed completely. The reason I say dissipates is because all compulsive gamblers continue to have stinky thinking from time-to-time, but they become stronger and more able to recognize it and secondly, not act upon it.

CHAPTER 3

THE LOSS OF PURPOSE

As I reflect on my descendance into stinky thinking and stinky action land, I believe I really lost the spirit of who I am when my marriage unraveled. I was always so good at keeping things together. I was very adept at keeping multiple balls in the air throughout my lifetime of gambling. I relished the opportunity to juggle so many balls at one time. The stress level of doing so was ridiculous. I'm sure it had some impact on my health in my twenties when I had bleeding ulcers since my body had trouble dealing with the mental abuse I put it through. In my mid-twenties I was in Cleveland, Ohio to work on annual budgets and my wife and kids decided to go with me. While they were at the hotel, I was at the regional office working on our budgets for the following year. I felt as if I had a flu bug. I was feeling weak, somewhat nauseous, not my normal self. I had no pain but didn't feel right. I remember going to the restroom and having a bowel movement which was black and tarry unlike I had ever seen before. After I came out of the restroom, I proceeded to spend the next four or five hours completing the budget process. Late that night I arrived at the hotel around 9 p.m. I got in bed shivering, thinking I have a full onslaught of the flu bug. As soon as I lay in bed, I had to immediately jump up and go to the bathroom. I had diarrhea. At least that's what I thought until I looked and saw the toilet bowl was filled with bright red blood. My immediate moves were to holler for my wife and then flush the toilet. I can only explain flushing the toilet as pure fear of seeing my blood filling it, knowing that I was bleeding heavily internally for some unknown reason. My wife comes in the bathroom and asks what's wrong. I told her I was bleeding. Since I had flushed the bloody bowl, I wiped my butt with toilet paper and the paper was bright red. My wife called 911 at that time and an ambulance was on its way to take me to Akron General Hospital.

When I was taken into the Emergency Room, they immediately sent a tube through my nose, down my throat and into my stomach. For the next six hours blood, red and black, were extracted through the tube from my stomach. Now I had no idea what the cause of my bleeding was, but it became evident to me that the hospital did. They believed it was cancer based on the doctors who were sent in and the questions they asked. The reason why I don't believe they considered ulcers to be the cause was that I had no pain from my stomach. No pain before, during or after the bleeding incident. The following morning my doctor did an endoscopy on me. As he was in my stomach with the scope, I remember him saying there's one, there's two, three, four and five. After he removed the scope out of my stomach and my mouth, he stated that he found five bleeding ulcers. All five had cauterized and were no longer actively bleeding. There I stayed in the hospital for the next two weeks. I didn't really understand why I had to be there for so long until after my first week, when the nurses allowed me up to shower for the first time in a week. I can remember the nurse walking me into the shower and then leaving me. As soon as the warm water hit me, I became dizzy and extremely weak. I went down to one knee in the shower, now recognizing why I had to be there for so long. My hemoglobin went down from 13 to 7 my first day in the hospital and it took me two weeks to regain my strength to properly function for myself, albeit at a noticeably slower pace.

Now when I look back at that time in my life, I view it as God trying to get my attention to stop my gambling. God wanted me to recognize that gambling was bad for me, my body, and my loved ones. I don't think I ever associated compulsive gambling as a factor with my bleeding ulcers. I probably did think that the stress of gambling played a role with my health, but if I did it was easier for me to place that blame on other people or in other areas. Even with all of that, I think where I truly lost it was when I realized my wife was serious about going through with a divorce. I can remember giving up on my marriage, giving up on who I was, and giving up on my belief of a reasonably happy life. I stopped making the house payment and paid only what I considered necessary bills, like loan payments from my gambling. Such stinky thinking infected me throughout that time. All of that is due to the insidiousness of this disease.

You must understand who I thought I was; why I thought I was put on this earth. The answer to both questions was to be a good father to my children and to set them up for success in their lives. Nothing was more important to me than my kids and their development. My wife was vitally important as well as she was the mother of my kids, and it was important to me for her to be happy and for me to make her happy. My kids are fine adults. Two of the three have children of their own. My ex-wife has moved on to create a better life with another man and without me.

Though there was nothing more important in my life than my family, I still could not stop gambling; no matter how badly I wanted to. Everything that I had planned to provide to my children and wife all went awry. This fact rocked me to my core for the next seven years until I landed at a Friday night GA meeting on March 4, 2011. At that point I was looking at prison, insanity, or death. If it wasn't for my kids and the impact my suicide would have had on them and their families over the course of their lives, I would have surely chosen death. I thought my life would never change, even with going to GA. Going to GA the first time in Chicago didn't stop me from gambling. I didn't believe going back to GA was going to stop me either, but what choice did I really have?

A funny, sad story from when I first met with my probation officer. He asked me if I had a drug or alcohol problem. I said no, I'm a compulsive gambler. He then said, "Too bad. If you did have a drug or alcohol problem, we could have sent you to rehab for treatment." To this day I still marvel in disgust at that statement. This is the plight of the compulsive gambler. A sad state of affairs, but the state nonetheless.

In 2004, I lost my reason for being or at least that is how I thought of it. My kids were still around; all of them were healthy. My ex-wife was moving on with her life. As I tried to do the same, I realized my purpose in life was lost. Now mind you, that was nothing but stinky thinking. My disease wanted me in its full control with no hope of ever putting Humpty Dumpty back together again. During this time, I found myself consumed on repairing the situation. Making up to my ex-wife and kids for the pain that I had caused them was my new purpose. What a convenient purpose. I was convinced the only way to achieve that was through hard work, taking care of things and gambling, of course. Again, there was the mistake.

There is no way to plan for anything when you are a compulsive gambler because you will always fall short on your plans. I truly believe that I was as addicted to bringing my wife and kids back together and resurrecting the family as I was to gambling. I thought that by getting my ex-wife back, that my kids would be pleased because I believed they wanted that as badly as I did. My kids are very intelligent though. They could see the strain and challenges my ex-wife and I had throughout our married life together. I was still gambling at that time. Although my new purpose was severely flawed, I could not see it. In my mind, I had to gamble to win back my losses for my newly found purpose to be fulfilled and all to be right with the world again.

Throughout that period when we would have family gatherings, my kids always had to worry about my ex-wife and my interactions during the event. Our time together at those family events was never comfortable, always contentious for whatever reason. She knew I wanted to bring the family back together and her take was, "Been there, done that." And who could blame her? Well, I could because I was still consumed in my own stinky thinking land. That should never be made into an amusement park. Nothing good goes on in stinky thinking land. These family gatherings would get me angry again, hurt my children, all of which I wanted no part of but was exactly what was happening.

I don't think I have mentioned my mother and father so far, so I need to include them. My dad was a hardworking man from southern Illinois where he grew up in pure poverty. His parents were so poor he was brought into the home of the Myers family in Jacksonville, Illinois and they took care of him so that he could graduate high school. He smoked three packs of Lucky Strikes a day all my life, and he liked to drink alcohol, but alcohol didn't like him. When drunk he would become mean which was exactly the opposite of his normal demeanor. He was a good man and a great dad. I love him very much. I lost him on June 30, 2010, at the age of 74. This hit me particularly hard. I wasn't ready for anything like this. When he went, it was quick.

I can remember having breakfast with my dad on a Saturday morning in April 2010, when we went to his bladder cancer doctor for results on his cancer operation. All the news was excellent, that the cancer was contained to the wall of the bladder and completely removed. We talked on how he had dodged such a big bullet and once again we looked forward to unlimited amounts of time together. Sadly, on Father's Day I had to drive from Michigan to Chicago as my dad had been readmitted to the hospital. I get to the hospital and within thirty minutes my dad's doctor comes in the room and breaks the news to us that the cancer had moved to his liver and lungs. Upon hearing this, internally I feel a rush of sweat, nervousness, adrenaline; an absolute ill feeling like I have never felt ever before. I spoke with the doctor outside the room to get more information from him and he told me how concerned he was that the cancer was in the liver. As he was saying this to me, the hallway began to spin as well as the doctors and nurses in it. I'm heating up, sweating, becoming nauseated and feeling like I'm about to go down. As the doctor continues talking, I let him know that I'm about to pass out and then he and a nurse take me over to a chair and give me some crackers and orange juice. Since that day I have not been able to truly enjoy a Father's Day and frankly, I don't know if I ever will. Weeks later my dad was dead, but if you could have seen his face when the doctor was telling him the cancer had spread to his liver. I believe that was the day my dad truly died. Not that he gave up, but he knew exactly what the doctor was telling him.

As you age you certainly do a lot of living and learning. Unfortunately for most, the learning is usually done the hard way. If I only knew then what I know now, I would have taken my dad out of that hospital and I would have brought him and my mom to live with me in Grand Rapids for him to get quality health care for his cancer at Spectrum Health. That is the same hospital/cancer center that performed my prostate cancer surgery. If I had done so, to this day I believe that my dad would have lived into 2011. That nine-month time frame between my dad's death and the date of my last bet, I believe, are no coincidence. The sudden downturn in my life, my finances, and my gambling went to new levels like never before.

My mom moved out of Chicago to live with me in Grand Rapids. I did my best to take care of her. She was on the rougher side. She was born in Lithuania, fled to Germany as a child during World War II and came over to Perry, Michigan for the family to work on a farm in order to stay in the United States. She moved to Chicago, met and married my dad, and became a United States citizen. My mother was also a hard worker. She was also a cleaning fanatic and you wanted to keep her on your good side. She could be tough, really tough. But she also had a heart of gold and would do anything for you. When my mother moved up by me, I quickly learned my mother liked what she liked and wanted what she wanted. All of that is usually in quick order. She was a compulsive gambler and she loved going to the casino. In a casino with thousands of slot machines, my mother would find three and throughout her entire gambling career at that casino, she would only gamble on one of those three machines. God forbid her three machines were taken because she would sit up and over the person on it until they finally took the hint and would seek out a different slot machine from the thousands that were available. My mother loved to gamble. If she had the money to do it 24/7, I think she would. Assimilating my mother into my bachelor lifestyle was difficult at times. She was still at the point of no one being good enough for her son, so bringing a girl back to my apartment wasn't a very good option. As we went to the casino while she was playing a couple of hundred dollars on the slot machines, I headed over to the roulette wheel and played thousands of dollars; that steady diet eroding both of our available funds.

When my embezzlement was found out on March 2, 2011, that ended my mom and my casino gambling escapades. I went from the first eight to nine months where my money was covering everything in our lives except my mom's gambling, to having to worry about how I am going to feed and house myself, let alone my mother. During this extremely difficult time, when I look at it now, I do believe that both my mom and I grew closer over going through such a difficult and nerve-wracking time together. She didn't get that I could not gamble again. She thought once we had money again, we could go right back to the way it was. But what I learned that turned out to be more important to my mom than gambling was eating. Did I previously say that my mom loved to eat? Well, my mom loved to eat. Her last couple of years of life I was my mom's food delivery service. Whatever she wanted, I was charged with getting it, and for the most part I did. We got along very well as I began to better understand my role in making her happy.

My Mom passed away on September 21st, 2014. In June of 2013 she was admitted to the hospital with pneumonia. When they checked her fluid lung cancer was found, and she was given 6 months to live. She lived 15 more months. Her first round of chemo went very well to the point where she was considered in remission back in February of 2014. Unfortunately, a couple of months later her cancer doctor ordered another CAT Scan and found the cancer was growing again. She had another 6 chemo treatments she could take before maxing out. She made it through two. I will never forget telling the physician assistant prior to her chemo treatment that something was not right with her after the first chemo treatment. They take bloodwork prior to the chemotherapy, and she was approved for the second chemo treatment, and then when her health declined after that treatment, we learned her liver, and kidney levels were off prior to the treatment. I still don't understand why they did not catch that prior to giving her the second treatment. The timing of her faltering was at the same time of my prostate cancer surgery. As my catheter is removed at the cancer center, then I walk across the street to visit my mom. Two weeks later my mom passes. For those of you that have lost your mom and dad I'm confident you understand the exceptional loss that you feel when your parents are gone.

Such a loss that there is no way for me to maximize its effect. It's one of the only times in my life that I have felt hollow. Like a was missing an appendage that I have carried around with me for the first 50 years of my life. For some reason I truly felt my parents would always be there. I can remember my wife and I talking about the days that would concern us most in the future. Top of the list was our parents passing, and yet the actual affect was so much worse. So there goes another shot at my purpose. As I'm going through my new One Day at A Time lifestyle, I began to think that maybe I was addicted to reuniting with my ex-wife and bringing the family back together when I was gambling. In recovery I was feeling that reuniting with my ex-wife was not the same compulsion that it was when I was gambling. No longer did I feel the necessity of us being together for me to bring my family together. My family were grown, and they were doing well in their own right.

Now at family gatherings my kids are no longer nervous about their mom and dad interacting together; at least that's what I'm feeling, and I'm thankful for that. I'm very thankful for that. So, what is my purpose now? I don't think there is any one thing. I think of my purpose as never gambling again, to take my disease to the grave with me dormant rather than active. That is important to me. Also being good for my kids, grandkids, hopefully around to experience great grandkids, Julie, our blended families, GA Family, and myself to experience the best that life has to offer would be a great purpose for me to live the rest of my life. A gambling free life.

CHAPTER 4

WHAT GAMBLING COST ME

A lot of people think that the primary cost of compulsive gambling is money. While loss of money is a significant cost, it's one of the smaller ones for a compulsive gambler. One of the largest costs to a compulsive gambler is time. You say what do you mean time doesn't cost you anything. When I was in gambling mode, I felt the same way. I never viewed the cost of time in my life. I treated it as a norm, as a way of doing business. I never calculated the time away from my wife, my kids, my friends, my other family members. I never calculated the time spent on stinky thinking; all of that time taken away from me. When I was in my twenties and thirties, I never thought of time. Now at 54-years-of-age, I recognize all the time I have lost to my compulsive gambling disease and that the time I have left on this earth is shortened considerably.

So, let's start with some of the costs of my gambling that occurred throughout my life. I was married twenty-one years to a very good woman. If I didn't gamble compulsively, I believe we would still be married. We were married young; many would say too young. We knew what people thought but I think we also wanted to prove some people wrong. One thing I want to make clear is that in my right mind, nothing was more important to me than my wife, my children, and my family. Lisa and I had many challenges throughout our marriage. I believe Lisa in time regretted getting married so young. I think a certain part of her would have preferred to go to college and have a career. I believe she blamed me at times for this. When we married, I was nineteen and she was sixteen, so I really couldn't fault her if she felt that way. I loved Lisa and I believe she loved me. The marriage, however, was a lot of work. Even though we were sexually compatible, in many other areas our compatibility was challenged. Our marriage was difficult, but I do believe we both tried our best to make things work. It would have been interesting to see how we would have been if I did not gamble. I think that would have improved our relationship immeasurably. I don't believe that would have ended the difficulty and ongoing challenges our relationship was faced with. Here's where I'm at with my ex-wife. I will love her forever and want nothing but the best for her. I have also realized that being with me is not what would have been best for her or me. It took two years of clean time for me to come to this realization. It's as though not only was I addicted to gambling, but also to Lisa as I wanted to get back together with her for seven years after the divorce. I felt the need to try and patch humpty dumpty back together again.

Trying to recoup your losses can keep a compulsive gambler gambling for decades. That happened to me. What amazed me was that between year one and two of my recovery, my obsession to get Lisa back and bring our family back together went away. What I learned what that as my obsession to gamble lessened, my need to make things right lessened as well. As that occurred my obsession of being with Lisa went away. Wow, what a difference.

Next on the time list to talk about was time lost with my kids. While I consider myself a good father, in all actuality I could have been a lot better. I believe I mentioned that compulsive gambling is a progressive disease. That proved to be so true as my children became older. I didn't notice time being an issue when my children were younger, but it certainly was as they became older. I was there when I could and should have been there. I didn't go out and gamble all day and night. When I gambled, I would go for an hour, pick my horses, bet them, and head home, and check the phone results the rest of the night. I could have given my kids more time and attention if I didn't gamble. I could have paid for my kids' college costs resulting in them not having to pay on any college loans if I didn't gamble. I wouldn't have asked them for or taken their money if I didn't gamble. I wouldn't have consistently hurt them emotionally if I didn't gamble. It is very difficult for me to believe the things I have done to my children with my gambling. Hurting my children along with my ex-wife are two debts that I will never be able to pay back or make right. Those issues alone kept me gambling for decades, thinking I could repair it with a big win. I was due. I should win back what I had lost.

Through recovery what I came to learn and believe is all my kids want for me is to be okay, to be able to take care of myself without negatively affecting them and to lead a good life. I doubt they had any faith that I would be able to quell this demon inside of me to live the life I'm currently living, and rightfully so because it's hard for me to believe it as well. So instead of trying to make up for the past, what I decided to focus on is that by not gambling today, I would be able to make up for my future as well as their future. So far, so good.

I can remember one of our GA members who used to tell me after my one-year anniversary that I should forgive myself. She would tell that to me repeatedly for an entire year. I would always respond, "I know what you're saying but I have done a lot of bad things to the ones I loved the most. Then she would say, "What about the pain you've inflicted upon yourself?" I would tell her that I felt that I deserved the pain that I inflicted upon myself, and that's the life of an addict. I thought that was simply the way my life was going to be. Even if I won, in time I would always lose. I knew it and near the end, I even expected it. What a crazy way to live, but that's exactly how I lived. I gambled for at least a decade simply based upon the loathing and disbelief that I had for myself. How could I continue to destroy myself along with consistently letting down my loved ones closest to me? Addicts of every kind do it on a daily basis.

One thing I talk about in GA is looking in the mirror, now versus then when I was gambling compulsively. When I gambled and would get home and after using the restroom, I can remember looking in the mirror and being just astonished at who and what was looking back at me. I thought I knew who I was but when I looked in the mirror, I knew my outward actions did not match my internal beliefs. I thought I was an honest, trustworthy, hardworking, family oriented and proud man. But when I looked in the mirror after a gambling event, I knew virtually none of that was true. I was a liar, a thief, not to be trusted or counted on, destructive to me and my family, and a lowlife, convicted felon. That is really what I saw and thought of myself when I used to look in the mirror. Very sad because I know there are so many good people who are compulsive gamblers and other addicts that, due to their disease, do dastardly things to themselves and, most especially, to their loved ones.

Aside from family and loved ones, friendships were also impaired by my compulsive gambling. Work as well as work relationships were strained as well as severed due to my gambling. During the a.m. I would plan who, what, and where I would bet that day. I would go to work. At some point I would run to the OTB (Off Track Betting) facility to play my horses for the day and then go back to work. I was always uneasy running to place bets during work hours, but I was insanely driven to do so. Even though I knew it was wrong, my compulsion was so great I would do it. I can remember being late for multiple business dinners because I wanted to collect from any a.m. winnings to play additional races in the evening. I did this seven days a week for decades. Again, the disease is progressive, so it took me decades of gambling to get to this point. In the beginning I would never go out to gamble during work hours.

One thing that I believe is consistent for compulsive gamblers is that you become enamored with yourself with all the lying and how easy it is for you to manipulate things, people, and circumstances. You admire your ability to control things even though your level of control is flimsy, at best. Ultimately, gambling almost cost me a major portion my life.

At my second GA meeting in Grand Rapids, Jim A. said he was convinced that gamblers of our type were in the midst of a progressive disease that would lead to either prison, insanity, or death. Those words continue to reverberate in my mind to this day. I hope they will forever. On March 3, 2011, I was looking at the real possibility of all three. I was convinced I was insane. Who has a good guy on one shoulder telling him what to do and a bad guy on the other shoulder doing the same thing? Prison was a very realistic possibility based upon my embezzlement from work, and death seemed to be my only option to stop hurting myself as well as other family members. Ultimately, after two weeks of taking a bath at 9:30 a.m. every day, carrying a large kitchen knife wrapped up in a towel to the bathroom with me and setting it down on the floor while I bathed, all I would do was think and hide. I would think about the knife. I would think about killing myself. At times I thought my family would be better off with me gone. Other times I thought that would be the easy way out for me, and that my kids would be adversely affected for the rest of their lives. Earlier I talked about the good guy on one shoulder and the bad guy on the other. Unfortunately, with an addiction it is difficult to impossible to determine which one to listen to. So, after two weeks of angst, I finally determined that killing myself would be easy for me and impossible for my loved ones. I decided to take what I considered the difficult road. I felt that I deserved to take the long and difficult road for all the things that I had previously done. The slow road. The road to recovery. I truly prayed to stay strong and not gamble again. Then my focus turned to simplifying that and making my mantra not to gamble today and to rebuild my new life.

I was very nervous and fearful for my new life, especially in my first year of recovery. I believed the best thing for me was to pay for my past mistakes. Whatever the judge determined the law required, along with work and quality of life ramifications, I intended to take life one day at a time. Not to gamble today, and to hope and pray that my life would improve from the massive crater I created in it. It took me two years of sobriety to finally get past blaming myself for all the wrongs I committed in my previous life; two years that frankly astonished me as I truly felt that I would never ever be able to forgive myself for all the bad I had done to negatively affect my children and other loved ones. What I learned was that I could not do anything about the past and my past mistakes. But I could do my very best not to gamble today, one day at a time, and see how my new life arose from the ashes I left behind from my old life.

CHAPTER 5

MY EARLY YEARS OF RECOVERY

The road to recovery is slow, ridiculously slow. You begin to live one day at a time, meaning all you must accomplish for that single day is not to gamble. That sounds simple. For a compulsive gambler it is anything but simple. It's extremely difficult to do and, in some cases, impossible. I can still remember how slow and difficult my first year of recovery was.

Recovery Year One - The Year of Fear

I was out of work for about a month and a half and, by the grace of God, I was offered a job at Walmart as an overnight stocker. I was hired in at minimum wage plus one dollar per hour due to working the overnight shift. I was so thankful to work again and be able to earn money to support myself. I went from a job of little to no physical exertion, to a job that was nothing but physical exertion. I had no car as I was renting at the time of my job loss and legal troubles. Thankfully, my youngest son Chris was living with me as he was midway through college. I was able to use his car most overnights. As he slept, I worked. If he needed his car, then I would take a cab. I was forty-eight years old at this time. I was overweight, five foot ten and two hundred thirty pounds. I began going to BioLife Plasma twice a week to earn money donating plasma. Talk about a change of life. I was confident and committed to work as hard as I could not to gamble again. My job and any other ego propping things were not only insignificant but were missing entirely. I truly felt as though I was in the fight of my life and no matter how difficult things were and were going to get, it was imperative for me not to gamble today. Unfortunately, as I would consistently tell myself that, I would also yearn to go and gamble. I attended GA meetings twice a week. Without a doubt during my first year and a half of sobriety, GA was my higher power. No matter my urgings to gamble, I went to GA, kept an open mind, while listening and learning more about the disease within me. Special thanks to Jim, Ernie, Carol, Dave, and any other GA member I encountered that first year that helped me move forward in recovery.

I worked for Walmart for about a year and a half. I worked my way up from part time to full time. Over the course of my first year at Walmart I lost forty to fifty pounds. I was down as low as one hundred eighty pounds which seemed too low, but I was thankful at the renewed energy I had. I was no longer winded running or walking any considerable distance. Year one of my recovery was a reboot for me physically and emotionally. I became more confident in my ability not to gamble today. I was in the best physical shape that I had been in over the past fifteen to twenty years of my life. What a blessing. I was beginning to see the benefit for my new life without gambling. Without question the job, coupled with going to BioLife Plasma twice a week to earn extra money, assisted me with my weight loss and getting back into shape. Committing to and going to GA twice a week assisted me greatly as I truly tried to take things one day at a time and to not gamble today. Meeting up with other GA members an hour or two before our Friday night meeting became a social event that I found myself looking forward to each week. This is going to sound crazy, but I was so pleased with myself and my growth in the program, as well as feeling like a human being again that I could afford spending two dollars each week at Denny's. I would always order their two-dollar eggs and hash browns or two-dollar biscuits and gravy meal. Add in another two dollars for the tip, and it would cost me four dollars and twelve cents, tip included, and I would be happy as a clam while headed to my Friday night GA meeting. That time at Denny's also reminded me of how many good people are affected with this destructive disease within their lives.

Throughout my first year of recovery, I can remember multiple times dreaming that I was gambling. These dreams would be so vivid and realistic. I truly felt I was there and that I was gambling. Normally when I dream, I realize that it is only a dream. However, these dreams I had that I went back to gambling were truly disturbing, yet mesmerizing. I could not believe that I was gambling again, yet here I am in the middle of the dream totally believing that I am gambling again and can't believe how I got there. How could I gamble again after all I had been through? The thought made me angry that I could be so foolish to throw away my recovery. I would then wake up in a major sweat. Sweat would be pouring from my body and it would take me some time to recognize that all of it was just a dream; that I had not gambled. This similar dream occurred on three occasions in my first year of recovery. Those dreams seemed so scary and real. I named year one as the year of fear based upon all the unknowns at the beginning of the year that would ultimately shape and direct the upcoming future of my new life. I was most fearful of gambling and that I would fall back into my disease. I really believed that I would be dead if I continued to gamble. I felt and continue to feel that my shelf life here on this earth was minimal if I ever went back to gambling. That was due to the progressiveness of the disease and my respect for it.

Recovery Year Two - The Year of Ben

Year two was a major concern of mine because ten years prior when I went to GA in Chicago for the first time and I was clean for twelve and a half months, I went back to gambling like a madman all over again. I did not want this to occur again, so it scared me. I believed it was important for me to work and complete the twelve steps of recovery for me in year two. I had a few people help me through working the twelve steps that year. Special thanks to Carol and Katie for all their assistance. During my earlier stint at GA, I worked the steps unsuccessfully as I was never totally committed to not gambling again and deep down, I knew that.

In my second year of recovery, I was buoyed by my daughter and then only grandchild, Ben, coming to live with me. They moved from the Chicagoland area to live with me and my mother in Grand Rapids. I was very pleased by my daughter's decision to move by me. I have always had what I consider to be a great relationship with my daughter. I was looking forward to them moving up by me. My daughter took an assistant teacher's position at a local school, while I became Ben's babysitter during the day. Ben was less than one year old. Mind you, I have never watched a baby in my life for more than one hour, let alone eight hours a day, five days a week. Even with raising three awesome children, my ex-wife was the one who did the heavy lifting of baby rearing. That doesn't mean I wasn't an active father, but I certainly didn't watch any of them as a baby for an entire day, let alone an entire year eight hours a day, Monday thru Friday. My days now consisted of watching Ben from 8:30 a.m. to 4 p.m. when my daughter would arrive back home from work. Then I would go to sleep and wake up at 9 p.m. to go to work at Walmart from 10 p.m. to 7 a.m. That was my life for the first six to seven months of recovery in my second year, not to mention that I continued with my BioLife Plasma donations twice a week and attending two GA meetings per week. That was enough to keep me focused, busy and exhausted.

Ben and I had a consistent pattern of what we would do Monday thru Friday. Our days consisted of the following: 8:30 a.m. – 10 a.m. watching VHI music videos. Around 10 a.m. I would make him breakfast. He liked me to fry him an egg. Around 10:30 a.m. I would take my daily shower and Ben would lay in his rocker and watch me. I would peek out from the shower curtain and say peek-a-boo. He liked that. He would eagerly await my popping my head out of the curtain to talk to him. By 11 to 11:30 a.m., we would make our daily trek to Sams Club where I would spend the next two hours pushing him around the store, talking to him, showing him different displays throughout the store. Ben especially loved the Beats headset and listening to the music that was playing on it. Ben enjoyed the samples at Sams Club and before we left, we would eat lunch together. He would either tell me it's pizza time or he would tell me to order him a dog-dog. So cute, so funny, and so memorable. One of the funniest things I remember is that I would talk to and with Ben the entire day until he would take his afternoon nap. Even when I couldn't understand what he was saying to me, I continued to talk to him like I did understand, and he would always talk back. I always looked forward to 1 pm. At that time, we would leave Sam's Club. I would put him in his car seat and drive him around until he fell asleep. That would usually take about five to ten minutes of driving before I would pull up at home and take him into the apartment and lay him down on his bed. Ben would usually sleep until three-thirty p.m., about thirty minutes before his mom came home, but occasionally he would sleep until she got home at four. Therefore, one p.m. to four p.m. was my time to rest while watching over Ben, and four p.m. to nine p.m. was my time to sleep and sleep I did. So, without question having my daughter and grandson with me during my second year of recovery had an immensely positive impact.

As my recovery was moving forward, I made a mistake that led to me getting fired from Walmart. I was crushed and fearful. As difficult as it was for me to find a job the first time with having a record, now I had to go through the pride crushing experience again. I didn't know what to do. I went online and I noticed that I was different this time around. Eighteen months ago, I would lie on the applications that I did not have a prior felony in hopes they would not do a background check on me. This time I completed the applications accurately with the thought process that I would be honest. Any compulsive gambler knows honesty is not our usual method for existing. A week later I was at my Friday GA meeting when I received a call from an unknown number, and they left a message. I had to use the restroom, so I listened to the voicemail. It was from the general manager of a pizza place that I applied to for a delivery position. I called him after the meeting, and we set up an interview for Monday. A week later I began work as a pizza delivery driver. I can remember being oh so thankful for the opportunity to work again. My hours became five p.m. to eleven-thirty p.m. during the week, and until twelve-thirty a.m. on Friday and Saturday nights. I was working full time and after about four to five months, I found that I was consistently making double what I had made at Walmart. Since I was no longer working overnights, I was able to get the proper sleep and rest I needed in watching Ben, as well as trying to live my life.

At this point in my life, I concluded that the mistake that got me fired from Walmart was not a mistake but divine intervention. In retrospect, there is no doubt in my mind what a blessing it was to have Ben with me and in my life. As I was trudging through the painstakingly slow road to recovery, here comes this beautiful little boy into my life. I didn't initially realize this was a time in which we may both have needed each other the most. I can say today without question that Ben sailed me through the second year of my recovery. I also worked on the twelve steps of recovery and completed them halfway through my second year. I felt that this achievement gave me the solid base I needed to resist the lifelong temptations I will have to gamble again.

Step One is etched in my mind and what I always refer to when stinky thinking permeates my mind from time to time. After completing my second year of recovery and all that I had been through in my first year, the fog of addiction, specifically compulsive gambling, was beginning to lift from consuming any part of my new life. I was two years into my new life, not even a toddler at this point and I was beginning to feel something that eluded me in my old life but was present in my new life. That something was hope; a life hopefully without gambling in it.

Recovery Year Three – The Year of Julie

After two and a half years of sobriety and being in another meaningless short-term relationship, I decided to stop dating for a year. I would work to improve my life and continue to not gamble again one day at a time. After six months of staying on course of not dating nor gambling, my life was improving. Still, I felt somewhat hollow. What I deemed most important in life was evading me. That was finding a woman, a good woman to share my life with and vice versa. After my divorce I dated often with no long-term girlfriends. Each one averaged anywhere from two weeks to two months. I am not a playboy, but I always tend to know what and who I like, and what I don't like as well. Also, I found with aging and having gone through a divorce, that relationship-wise I can be rather difficult. My longest relationship after my divorce was six months. We were compatible in many ways, and I did care for the woman, but I learned she was bipolar the hard way and away I ran.

My abstinence from dating lasted eight months. I remember at around seven months while on a pizza delivery, praying to God for me to find my soulmate. I prayed to find a woman who is kind, decent, trustworthy, attractive, and the yin to my yang. I was tired of being with someone just to be with someone. I missed the feeling of love for a woman, butterflies in my stomach and the feeling a teenager gets with a new love. Even though I truly believed I was on the right course, my life still felt extremely hollow being without what I needed most.

After seven months of not dating, for some reason I was compelled to reopen my eharmony account. I instructed my youngest son, Chris, to take my picture on my phone so I could load it onto eharmony. It was more like I was pleading with him to do so. I stood in front of a white door in my apartment and voila, I had my picture. Shortly afterward I began communicating with a woman that I remember very little about except that where I answered nothing that eharmony indicated that I should, she answered everything and then some. My belief in dating was always that you must meet a person face-to-face, communicate and see what happens. I did not consider myself a computer guru. After several days of communicating back and forth, the eharmony woman decided to make a date with me so we planned to meet at a park in Rockford, Michigan.

I arrived at the park on a Sunday. I see her and she brought a picnic basket. We went into the park and sat down at a picnic table. I remember thinking she was cute and a little nervous about jumping back into the dating world after being widowed. We ended up spending a good deal of time talking and got along rather well. The funniest thing I remember is her opening the picnic basket which I swear to this day had over one hundred dollars worth of prepackaged food in it. I was shocked at all the food she brought. I thought it was cute and sweet. I also thought she wasted about ninety-six dollars as I was too nervous to eat, and I thought she was as well. I mean this basket was loaded with food and it was a six-person family basket. I still chuckle at this as to what she was thinking in picking up all that food. We ate virtually none of it, but I found myself having a wonderful conversation with what I was beginning to think was a very intriguing woman and I could not explain why.

Julie then decided to show me a new area, Pickerel Lake Park which is wooded and beautiful. We walked over to the wooded area and walked some trails. Julie and I had our first kiss. Immediately after as we continued to walk Julie informed me the kiss was okay but nothing spectacular. I thought her response was a bit odd, but I was confident in my kissing ability and knew time would resolve any issues she may have with my ability to kiss. When I first kissed her, I intentionally held back not wanting to be overly forward and to break the ice and tension. She also informed me that I was not her type. At that point I was confused. I didn't like the "not my type" comment. We continued walking and got ready for our second kiss. That kiss was different for Julie. No more comments after that kiss about it not being much or not being her type. It appears Julie was liking what she was learning. After a few more kisses along a mile walk, we came to the end of the wooded walkway and as we were talking Julie tells me she plans to do a background check on me. I respond by telling her that she would find that I was a convicted felon, guilty of embezzlement in my former job and a compulsive gambler.

What is amazing to me about my response was one, that I actually said all of that, and that I said it calmly and honestly knowing that my honesty was likely to end this short-term romance. You must understand that as a compulsive gambler, one of the personal characteristics that take over your life is lying. I mean lying on a consistent basis, even when lying is not necessary. As a compulsive gambler you lie. It's almost as if it is easier to lie than to tell the truth. You know it is wrong to lie, but you do it anyway even though you know it's wrong. It's a vicious cycle. Then you must remember the lies you've told to continue to be consistent with your lies, an absolutely terrible way to live. I hated it but I did it when I gambled. However, I was pleased that I told the truth after Julie asked me what she would find if she did a background check on me. I told her the truth without a hint of a lie. This was new for me and made me feel good that my recovery was real and moving forward. I cannot tell you how much strength that situation provided me with my recovery.

Once I told Julie my reality, you can imagine the effect of the lead balloon that I had just delivered to her. I'm confident she was wondering how she could be in this wooded park area with me and was concerned with what she learned. Then we walked posthaste back to her car and then she dropped me off by my car. We talked a bit before I went to my car, but it was obvious the mood had changed. I let her know I had a great time and would like to see her again, even though I knew the chances of that happening were slim to none.

After my date I called my daughter Nikki and she asked me how my date went. I told her, "Well, I just had a picnic lunch with a woman who could have been your future stepmother, but unfortunately I don't believe she will ever be able to allow it to get to that point based upon my revelation when prodded that I was a convicted felon." For some reason I had this feeling that I had met the woman for me. As a compulsive gambler, you are used to things not going your way. So even though I believed she was the woman for me, I was confident she would not allow herself to believe that I could be the man for her. Julie and I continued to talk, however. She informed me that her daughters suggested that she should give me a chance and I think that surprised her when she told both of them my situation. She also had run a background check at home, and it verified everything I had told her.

I felt a little better that she might give us a chance, so I invited her to a Daughtry and Lifehouse concert coming up in a couple of days. I owe an apology to my son, Chris, who was to attend the concert with me, but thank you to Julie for agreeing to go, with the caveat that we would go just as friends. In fairness, I was the one who brought up going as friends to the concert, and that was because I didn't believe she would go otherwise based upon our previous discussions. So, Julie agrees to go and we go to the concert as friends, of course. Ugh! The concert is great, we like one another. I feel even stronger she could be the woman for me. I know she likes me. I can feel it.

Before the concert I told my daughter, Nikki, everything to date and she assured me Julie liked me and would kiss me again at the concert. So, at the concert we loved listening to Lifehouse and Daughtry. Unfortunately, no kiss. Julie intentionally tried to keep our time together almost on a professional basis. We had a great time though. As we walked to her car and got inside, I knew she was going to want a goodnight kiss. We got into her car and I listened to her say how good the concert was and that we were just friends. Somehow, I felt I had just entered the friend zone and I did not know how. How could I be feeling all the romantic feelings about her with her feeling only friendship for me? I was at a loss and it was making me crazy.

On my drive home from the concert, I pulled into the parking lot of my apartment complex and called Julie. I told her I couldn't continue as friends, that I had romantic feelings for her, and this friend zone thing was too difficult emotionally for me continue with. Then, to my surprise, after reminding me the friend zone was my idea, she seemed to move off just being friends. I disputed it had been my idea as I had only mentioned it so we could get together as friends so she would get to know me better and learn that I am a good man.

I made an actual romantic date for me to come to her house after work a couple of days later. That night we basically blew the roof off the relationship. Our romantic feelings for one another erupted into a couple hours of pure, unadulterated passion. The following day while I was working the late-night shift and Julie calls to tell me that she was meeting a guy the following day for coffee. She told me her daughter set it up and out of respect she was going to meet the gentleman so she could tell her daughter she met with him. After hearing that and thinking it through, it took me about five minutes to figure out that wouldn't work for me. I called Julie to let her know that and that I couldn't believe after the night we just had that she would entertain the thought of dating someone else. I told her we couldn't move forward if she was going to do this. It was like high school all over again. I was nervous, sick to my stomach, had a headache, and was angry that she would have the audacity to let me know she was going out on a date with a different man, after what I thought we shared the night before. I go to bed that evening feeling as if the relationship was over, and that Julie was not the type of person I thought her to be.

Anger, disappointment, nervousness, and lack of control were all symptoms that when I was gambling would get me to gambling immediately. I would feel in control when I was gambling. I never liked that fact or admitted that I couldn't control my gambling. For all the years I gambled I always felt that I was in control. I was doing what I wanted to do, and nobody was going to stop me. My disease would consistently feed me that narrative for me to remain strong in my disease, rather than show weakness by not gambling. It took well over a year of clean time for me to recognize what a crock of crap that thought process was. But that's what this disease does. It makes you think wrong is right and what is right is wrong. It's amazing how convinced I was with this throughout my years of compulsive gambling. All I can do now is simply shake my head at how much stinky thinking was going on in my mind when I gambled, and how I acted like I was programmed to do wrong and believe it was right. Anyone with an addiction, I believe understands this perception all too well. Even though we have different vices, one commonality is that we are all besieged with stinky thinking which alters our perception of reality.

Back to my early dance with Julie. I was deeply hurt and disappointed. I didn't sleep very well, needless to say. Around 10:30 a.m. the following morning I received a phone call from Julie. She informs me that she wasn't going out for coffee and that she didn't know what she was thinking and had not been looking at the meeting as a date and that she only wanted to be with me. That worked for me, as I only wanted to be with her. But I'll admit, I felt the need to be more cautious as I learned more about Julie over time. From that time on moving forward, it seemed the angst that Julie was struggling with had been removed. She also asked for my sponsor's phone number. When she called Jim A., they had a good conversation and Julie felt secure that I was not gambling. Other than my own relationship issues causing questions between our fifth and sixth month together, life with Julie has been an absolute blessing. What I mean by my own relationship issues is that since my divorce I had only been with one woman for six months, everyone else less than a month or two. So around five months, I began to believe that I would do something to mess the relationship up and that I may not be capable of another long-term relationship after my wife of twenty-one years divorced me due to my compulsive gambling. What was funny is a day after Julie and I reached our six-month anniversary together, I straightened up. No longer was I worried about messing our relationship up.

What I have learned about Julie in my recovery years from three through six is that Julie is one of the best women

I have ever met. Her love and devotion for me is without question. I feel it and I feel her. Julie is uniquely different than I am. Julie truly cares about people. I care about my family members and close friends. I remember when she first informed me of her volunteer work. I would always ask her how much she was getting paid for it. I always tell her that she is a better person than me. I do believe that I'm a very good person, but she is much better than I. Life with Julie for me has been so easy. We rarely ever fight, argue, or have harsh words. My past relationships were filled with too much verbal bickering and general unhappiness. Julie sits in on my GA meetings, not to keep me in check but to learn about the disease as well as supporting the rest of the group. All I want for Julie is the best. She deserves it. I assure you this book is not meant to be a love story, but I would be remiss in my new life and discussion of recovery without mentioning the enormous effect my relationship with Julie has had on me and what it has added towards my sobriety. You must understand that I prayed exactly for this woman two months prior to meeting her. I prayed not to date another woman just to only have a short-term relationship. I wanted a relationship with meaning. As a romantic, I wanted the ideal woman for me and that is who God provided me.

Recovery Year Four - The Year of Prostate Cancer and My Own Mortality

In January of 2014, for the first time in over three years I went into my doctor for a physical. It was the first year of the Affordable Care Act and I was able to obtain health insurance for the first time in over three years. My total monthly payment was less than thirty dollars a month for Blue Cross Blue Shield which was a blessing. I decided to go in for a physical. Everything went fine and I was just waiting on my blood test results. I felt fine; no serious reason to see the doctor other than I was over fifty and had not been to see him in the over three years in which I had no insurance.

About a week after my visit, I received a call from the nurse, notifying me that my prostate specific antigen (PSA) was 4.2 and that my doctor was referring me to see a urology specialist. I received this information, not knowing anything about what a PSA test was even for and then I did the next logical thing and googled it, learning that I had prostate cancer or could have, among other things. As I continued to read, I found every opinion under the sun as to what a 4.2 PSA test meant. I was scared and confused when I was finally able to see the urology specialist in April. The specialist did his best to calm my fears. He told me we would take it a step at a time and to start with, he would redo the blood test. About a week later I learned my latest PSA came out to 5.1 but, more importantly, the specialist did what they call a PSA free test and that was the number that I eventually learned concerned the doctor. The nurse called me a week later with the results and to schedule a prostate biopsy. I had about three weeks between learning of this next step and the actual procedure. When the three weeks were up, I was not ready for the biopsy based upon all my internet learnings regarding prostate cancer and the biopsy procedure. I went to the specialist for a consultation. I told him my concerns and to learn why a biopsy was necessary. He explained to me that the PSA Free test number was what concerned him. In fact, he stated he has never seen anyone not have prostate cancer with the PSA free number I had. I recognized that I had played physician's assistant (PA) long enough and scheduled the biopsy procedure two weeks later.

If you listen to Howard Stern, Ronnie the Limo Driver will tell you how bad the prostate biopsy procedure is. I didn't find it as bad as Ronnie did, but I also would not recommend it if it was not a necessity. First the area is numbed and then the prostate is given multiple shots to deaden the pain of the biopsy. The procedure lasted about twenty to thirty minutes and I honestly didn't feel any pain until the last five minutes when the final three biopsies were taken. The doctor said the deadening agent was probably wearing off and asked if I would like him to desensitize the area again. I said no and handled the uncomfortability for the remainder of the procedure.

About a week later I received a call directly from my specialist. It's funny now, but when I realized I was talking to my urology specialist for this call, prior to him saying anything I knew I had cancer. Up until hearing his voice on the phone, I truly believed that I did not have cancer. I always viewed myself as healthy and indestructible. No way could I ever have cancer. But as soon as I heard his voice and that he was the one calling me, I knew I had cancer. I'm driving in my car listening to the longest shortest conversation from my specialist telling me that I had cancer. He told me where it was and told me of a Kelvin scale that showed it as four plus three totaling seven. Since it was an aggressive form of prostate cancer based upon the scale, in June they set me up for a half day of reviewing my case, my cancer, and making the best decision on how to treat my condition. This could have consisted of surgery or removing the prostate, radiation therapy, or to monitor the numbers. Due to the aggressiveness of my cancer, monitoring did not seem to be a viable option. I spent half a day meeting with my urology specialist, cancer radiation doctor, and general cancer doctor one-on-one. I then went before a mini board of specialists for a short meeting to provide their recommendation to me for treatment. After meeting with each of them, I was pro surgery to remove the prostate and to remove it robotically as my hospital had a doctor who specialized in the robotic procedure. The major reason for my wanting the robotic procedure was due to healing time. I would be off work two to three weeks instead of the four to six weeks for the traditional prostate removal procedure. I was told to contact their scheduling office to set up the surgery date and time.

Their first opening was around seven weeks later at the end of July, and Julie and I had some concerts scheduled in July and August. Therefore, I set the appointment up for the first week of September. Julie was not happy with me over that one. She thought I was putting my life in jeopardy to go to a concert. I reminded her that wasn't the case. I asked the doctor and he said I would need it done prior to December and that September would be fine. Plus, it was KISS and Def Leppard in July, followed by the Goo Goo Dolls in August, and I had never seen the Goo Goo Dolls before. I will admit that a three month wait to have your cancer surgery is an incredibly long wait. But I will also say that after the Goo Goo Dolls concert in late August, one week prior to my scheduled surgery I walked out of that concert thoroughly fulfilled and ready to tackle the cancer within me. I went from scared and concerned to being ready and aggressive to tackle what was before me. I had faith in God that he would not give me more than I could handle and that he would heal me.

September came and I went in for my surgery. I was taken into the operating room and the nurses began to shave me while my anesthesiologist is above and just behind me, and my cancer surgeon is stationed five to seven yards across the room. Before I go to sleep, I'm thinking that's a long way away, but I did have confidence in him and the robotic procedure. One major reason I was so pro the robotic procedure was my dad would always say that when air hits the cancer, that is when it spreads. I was concerned about the cancer spreading and felt the robotic procedure was the least invasive and that the air hitting it would not be an issue. About three hours later I wake up in the recovery room feeling pain from my bladder spasming. Mind you, I didn't know that's what was causing the pain. I told the nurse and she proceeded to insert a suppository into my rectum. I just laid there, wondering what the hell that was all about. On the good news side, my pain went away, and I was thankful to be awake again and out of surgery, seemingly in one piece. Four hours later I was walking the hallways of the urology wing, on my feet and up and about. Other than occasional spasms, I was surprised by the lack of pain I felt afterwards. My PA came into my room before my walk to check me out, and that's when I learned I had a tube inserted into my bladder. But I felt good and thankful, along with being worried about what the prostate results would show in a week. It was also the first time I had a catheter in me. That concerned me as much as anything as I was afraid I would roll over and tear it out, and I thought the pain of removing it would be incredible. I felt this way going back to my June meeting where my doctor told me that the day of removing my catheter would not be one of my favorite days. I had no idea what that meant other than I was in for a painful experience.

I was discharged from the hospital the following day and the following week I went to see my PA to have the catheter removed and to find out what they learned from dissecting my prostate and the state of my cancer. I'm extremely nervous the day of and I enter the exam room. The nurse comes in and says, "Let's take that catheter out." I'm thinking, "Where's the PA or doctor, or someone other than this nurse who is going to see me breakdown from all the pain of removal?" In conversation, I mentioned my urology doctor telling me this would not be one of my favorite days or experiences. The nurse seemed stunned the doctor would say that to me. She told me there would be no pain removing the catheter. I took a "time will tell" approach to her comment. Fifteen seconds later the catheter was out, I didn't even know it and she was true to her word; no pain at all. Now I don't know what it feels like going in as they placed the catheter in when I was unconscious before the surgery, but I can tell you for me on removal of the catheter there was absolutely no pain. I also learned that there was a minimal amount of cancer that had potentially escaped out of the prostate. My PA made me feel as comfortable as I could be with that fact, stating that the amount that potentially had bled out, he believed, would have most certainly been destroyed by the cauterization process the surgeon used upon removal of the prostate and cauterizing the surrounding areas.

Next was a one month wait to see my surgeon, take a new PSA test to determine if the cancer had spread outside the prostate and to learn my fate. When I arrived for my appointment, the PA told me that my PSA was below any level of concern. I felt so fortunate and thankful to hear that. I would have to continue with every six-month PSA testing along with annual visits to my PA. I was fine with that. After my google investigation regarding the disease, I was sure traces of PSA would remain and that I would have to undergo radiation therapy in order to get the rest of the cancer. Thankfully, that was not the case.

I will never forget the feeling I had when my urology doctor first told me that I had cancer. It seemed very similar to a couple of earthquakes I was in while in California in the nineteen eighties. At the beginning everything went silent around me, then suddenly, a rush of wind came forward as the doctor told me that I had cancer, and then all hell broke loose within my mind and afterward I was left numb from what I just heard and the reality of it all, and what that could potentially mean for me and my life. Geez, what a feeling; a feeling I would not wish on anyone. For a short time I felt lost within myself. Then God took over and reminded me that He was in control, and to welcome the lack of control over my life instead of fearing it. This took me awhile, but I eventually relished the fact that what God decided for me I would follow. If you knew me before my gambling recovery, that belief from me would shock you. I truly felt thankful for all that I had in my life. I had a wonderful woman, my children, my grandchildren, my GA family, good friends, a good job, and I felt good physically, even with my condition. I recognized many people out there were suffering daily, and not reaching their full potential of what God has in store for them. I was truly fortunate for all that I had. What an interesting learning for me at this point in my recovery: another challenge personally but one that made me more thankful for what I had and made me stronger in wanting to continue to improve my quality of life, to help others, and to appreciate the life that I had.

CHAPTER 6

THE POWER OF MUSIC IN MY RECOVERY

I find that music affects me in many ways. It always has. I love music. It speaks to me. In my second year of recovery, I was laying out in the sun one day and I had an epiphany to lead a GA meeting centered around music and how I viewed myself through songs and their lyrics. I contacted the leader of my Monday night meeting and obtained approval to lead the next meeting. I went out to a Best Buy and bought a forty-dollar boom box and bought two compact discs with the songs I had chosen for Old Al, the gambler, and New Al, the recovering gambler. The song I chose for Old Al was "Bring Me to Life" by Evanescence and for New Al I chose "Shadow Days" by John Mayer.

I handed out the lyrics to everyone at the meeting and I started off by playing "Bring Me to Life" by Evanescence. If you've never heard the song before, I would strongly encourage you to listen to it. Number one, it's a great song. Number two, this song speaks to me as a compulsive gambler. It's as if this song was my life as a compulsive gambler. The line "wake me up inside, I can't wake up" so spoke to me as a gambler. "Save me from the nothing I've become" was that end of the night feeling while looking at myself in the mirror. I could never understand how I got to this point. It was impossible for me to see the destructive nature of my disease, not only financially but emotionally as well. It was like my disease wanted me to feel bad, to fail until I got to the point of self destruction. That was what I believe my disease wanted from me. That was its end game, and then it could move on to someone else. I was crying out internally to be woken up inside from this life and I couldn't wake up to stop gambling. Then "save me from the nothing I've become" was me, was what I had become. All my concerns and fears with my gambling had come true. I had become nothing, and I felt like that from years of gambling compulsively. What a sad place. What a sad existence. What's even sadder is the number of people who continue in their addictions today and the negative effect it has on them and their families. I so know that horrible feeling. For me, when I was presenting this to other members, I was actually very positive of the fact that this is the song story of my gambling life.

"Shadow Days" was the song of my recovery. "Shadow Days" hit me at the very beginning of the song. "Did you know that you could be wrong and swear you're right. Some people been known to do it all their lives." Wow! Isn't that the truth. You could be wrong, swear you're right and do it all your life. That was me when I gambled. It was so me. I absolutely love those lines now that I'm in recovery. They speak to me. When I gambled, I would swear what I was doing was right. I never thought of being wrong or that I was doing wrong, though deep down I knew what I was doing was the wrong way to live. Doing it all my life was what I thought my life would be. I never truthfully believed that I would ever be capable of stopping gambling because, honestly, it was all that I knew.

"I found myself in pieces on the hotel floor" was another line in the song that spoke to me. Have you ever been to that point about anything in life? I have. Gambling and divorce are two things in my life that brought me to my knees. The divorce was primarily due to my gambling. Such powerful words, "You find yourself alone like you found yourself before, and I found myself in pieces on the hotel floor." Again, Wow! Those words really hit me to my core. It's an enormous effect on a person to have a disease that you don't know is a disease and that you view as what should be a controllable weakness. I know my disease wanted me to view it in that manner, so that I would feel bad, to confirm my belief that I was a bad person, even though deep down in my heart I knew that wasn't so. Unfortunately, the negative feelings of my disease would nearly always win out. Those feelings would make me want to repair the situation by doing the same thing repeatedly to obtain a different result. Yet the same result would always occur. Sounds like the definition of insanity to me and when in my disease that was certainly true, even though I could never see it that way.

Hard times truly did help me see, and now I truly believe that "I am a good man with a good heart." I had tough times and rough starts. I finally learned to let it go. So true. Thank God. That is one of the most impactful lines for me, "But I finally learned to let it go." That is something which I never truly believed I would ever see. Such a blessing and such beautiful words. Words of hope. For me, this song is an anthem of hope. When I gambled, I very rarely thought of myself as a good man. I don't think my disease wanted me to think that I was. I believe I gambled longer and harder based upon my belief that I wasn't the good man that I wanted to be and that I thought I was. I'm hoping that my "shadow days" are over. I had hoped that for decades prior, but for some reason while fairly new to recovery, I was hopeful that my "shadow days" were over and now I believe they are over. Knowing, however, that I will have to take it one day at a time and work the program.

After listening and discussing both songs with GA members, I noted the stark difference in the music styles of both songs. What I mean is, if you listen to "Bring Me to Life" you will hear a raw, raucous, emotional, pleading, screaming, praying, loud rendition of my troubled life of gambling. As frenetic as the song is when listening to it, my life of gambling was no different. What a powerfully moving song amidst the chaotic life of a compulsive gambler. I would be supercharged simply listening to it. One thing I didn't touch on with "Bring Me to Life" was the effect of the words, "Wake Me up, I Can't Wake Up" which was so true to how I felt when I gambled, and I so desperately wanted to stop. For decades of my life there was nothing I wanted to do more than stop gambling and still I couldn't. I truly felt that I would never wake up. The angst of the song and its lyrics felt like my life to me. As much as "Bring Me to Life" would rev me up, the same could be said for how "Shadow Days" calms me and makes me smile. Along with making me smile as I listen to the song and sing it for a while, tears will fill my eyes as I look back on the road that has finally taken me to this peaceful place in my life.

The following song impacted me both negatively as well as positively in my recovery, "What I've Done" by Linkin Park. This song had multiple meanings to me at different times of my recovery. In the beginning I would be saddened by the song's lyrics for all the bad that I had done. Then as my recovery continued, my take on the song lyrics changed as well to where I would rejoice in communicating, "And whatever pain may come, today this ends, I'm forgiving what I've done." I believe holding onto the pain of your past will keep you remaking those same mistakes. But true growth lies in recognizing that you must overcome the destructiveness of your past, and that your past does not have to rule your future. Everyone talks about learning from our mistakes, but how many of us really do? I'm sure you know people in your lives who are on their own quasi merry-go-round, rollercoaster ride they call life.

Finally, you listen to the song, "Show Me What I am Looking For" by Carolina Liar and you hear a song that is totally opposite the anthem from my gambling days. It is a warm, smooth, loving, mellow, comfortable, and calm song that befits how I feel in recovery. This song was crucial to my recovery, short- and long-term. I first heard this song on the television during my first year of recovery. The instant I heard it I was affected by it. What a song for me at the time of my life that I was in. I will never forget it. Of all the song lyrics that I've mentioned in my book, this song without question had the biggest impact on me and my recovery. For the song to come out in the first year of my recovery was a blessing. Its words were exactly what I needed. I can remember going from teary-eyed to outright bawling while listening to it throughout my first year of recovery. Now mind you, I'm not a crybaby by any means, but when you have lived the life that I have and I know so many people who have, it's hard not to be affected by your plight in life and how you got there. This song is and was an anthem of hope for me. It came to me when my life was a complete mess. I had forsaken everything and everyone for my gambling disease, and I was brewing in the stew of mess that I had made of my life. This song began a slow recovery in my faith of God. I can't tell you how I prayed, hoped, scratched, and clawed that first year to not gamble today. In the beginning this song reminded me of my regret but, as my time in recovery lengthened, it gave me hope for my future. I would cry out to God to show me what I'm looking for, to guide me on where I should go and what I should do. You must understand that in year one of my recovery, the old me was absolutely destroyed. I used to be confident that I could do anything and control it as well. That was a lie.

The new me in year one of recovery was someone who was broken, scared, nervous, unsure, and lacked confidence. I wasn't confident that I could be repaired. "Save me, I'm lost" was me for the first year and a half of my recovery. All I wanted to do was not to gamble, not to hurt myself, not to hurt any of my loved ones, to do the right thing and to stay out of trouble. "I've learned to love abuse" is another line that reinforces my belief that my addiction wanted the worst for me. "Mistakes become regrets, I learned to love abuse" was sure to keep me gambling.

"Show Me What I am Looking For" helped me to seek out God. Throughout my first year of recovery the Lord had not awoken within me yet. Now I'm embarrassed to say what I used to say at times in my first year of recovery at GA, that I felt like God had forsaken me. I viewed myself as a bad reality TV show that God loved to watch. All my dealings and shenanigans had to be entertaining to someone who did not care about me. The lyrics, "Should have done better than this" were so true to me and the point I was at in my life. I felt like a failure. I felt as if my life was over. I felt as if I had lost. So, "Show me what I'm looking for" was an anthem for me. In my first year of recovery, I was just trying to remain alive, to not do anything that I would regret and, most of all, not gamble today. I would pray to God to show me the way, to light up the path because I was flawed and unable to do it on my own. "Oh Lord, I've been waiting for you" was such a true statement. At the time I wasn't fully there for God, but I knew I wanted to be. The only question was how do I get there?

I began to believe that I needed to give up control of my life and turn that over to God. So, I did and over the years, time and time again I was shown that was the right decision. It took me a little over a year to recognize the truth. God had never forsaken me; it was I who had forsaken Him. No more. I repeat, no more! What I came to realize was that He had been with me my entire journey back to Him and the light.

God does offer free will, so I had to do a better job with the choices I was making. He also helped me to see things differently than I ever had when I was in my compulsive gambling mindset. The fact remains that I cannot listen to this song without tearing up, thanking God for righting me and my life.

You can choose to believe that things just happen, God exists or he doesn't, or that you simply hope he exists. For me I know he exists. There were so many crossroads during my recovery that required me to make the correct turn, and repeatedly I made the right decision. There is no doubt in my mind that God had and has my hand to guide me toward taking the right path for the type of life He wants, and I want for me. God chose to show me time and time again that He was there for me. I feel good about who I am now and the choices I make; the things I do. I can remember first listening to this song and how it impacted me. It made me feel so thankful to God for getting me to the point in my life to where I could hear and understand those words. Also, I became convinced that I was indeed the good man with a good heart that I always thought I was which made me feel good. I went through this music exercise at the GA meeting for people to feel what I feel. I wanted them to recognize the disparity and recklessness that the life of gambling provides and to compare it to the peace of recovery.

The difference for me in year two of my recovery versus year one was that I recognized, could see, and feel that God was truly in my life. "I'll pay any cost" and "Save me from being confused" I would sing to Him every time I heard this song, as if I was praying it out loud. I truly meant that I would pay any cost. I think that's one of the things that assisted me in getting through my first couple of years of recovery where my new life was very challenging in so many ways than my prior life had been.

"Mistakes become regrets; I've learned to love abuse." Wow, so powerful. If you're a compulsive gambler, you feel the impact of that statement. "I've learned to love abuse" I think is so consistent with anyone fighting an addiction. Nobody loves abuse but compulsive gamblers sort of do when you think about abuse. The amount of abuse we impart upon ourselves and our lives with our actions is staggering. There's no doubt that my disease loves my abuse. It yearns for me to have it. That's when it is most happy. Frankly, I thought I deserved all abuse that might me bestowed upon me. "Save me, I'm lost, Oh Lord I've been waiting for you." Truer words were never spoken. The impact of those words upon me and my recovery were profound and still are to this day. I will never forget screaming out to God to save me, admitting I was lost, and pleading to Him that I've been waiting for Him. You must understand that in my gambling diseased mind, I wouldn't have the time to even notice something God would do for me. I was so focused on gambling I was blind to everything and everyone else around me. "Wait, I'm wrong, I can't do better than this" would lift me up when I heard that part. It made me feel blessed that I had reached the point in my life to where my disease was dormant within me, God was front and center, and that my life was moving forward consistently. I had jumped off the crazy train and survived. Of course, early on I was battered and bruised but not down or out. Thank God.

CHAPTER 7

JUMPING OFF THE CRAZY TRAIN

When I refer to jumping off the crazy train, I'm talking about stopping gambling. Life as a compulsive gambler is like being on a constant roller coaster ride filled with various highs and insurmountable lows. What's amazing is that I don't like heights or roller coaster rides, but I lived my life on one for over four decades. I often speak at GA meetings about how long I rode the crazy train of gambling. As a compulsive gambler, you must do everything fast otherwise how could you explain all of the dumb decisions of going out and gambling night after night after night. There is no way a compulsive gambler could function with a slow thought process because you would know that you were destroying your life and that would be crazy. Compulsive gambling is oh so fast each day and night, speeding by into the next one.

Recovery is oh so slow. Each day takes forever in the beginning, as do the nights. I think this is why it is so difficult for a compulsive gambler to stop gambling. The change in lifestyle is so uniquely different, virtually worlds apart. At the beginning of recovery all compulsive gamblers want a quick fix. They want for each day to go by fast and for them to find another activity to absorb themselves into which gives them the same high that compulsive gambling provides, but with none of the problems compulsive gambling causes. Unfortunately, there is no such thing. When you tell this to a new GA member, you can see the winds of hope leave their sails. By speaking the truth, it's like you took away the only hope that they brought with them. When they begin to realize how long and lonely the process of recovery will be, the vast majority fall back to the wayside and back into their disease. This is another negative of having this dastardly disease. It takes your hopes and dreams. It lies to you on a constant basis.

One of the most important learnings in recovery is to slow down. You must work really hard to slow your life down. Slow down your thought process, slow down on trying to do too much. Your only focus should be on not to gamble today. Now with saying all of that, I can't express how difficult it is to do this. For me it was like, how do I turn off over forty years of behavior all at once. I wanted to find something to take my mind off each and every long, slow day. GA, coupled with work and not gambling today, became my areas of focus. I thought going to GA twice a week would help time move forward, and that it would also be good for me to hear from other compulsive gamblers.

This mindset makes me think about a certain GA meeting I was at where we had a compulsive gambler who was going to thirty meetings in thirty days. That is what he was going to do to stop gambling. He was so sure it would work. By the fourth week he opened up that he was doing the thirty meetings in thirty days because the judge in his pre-sentencing court date recommended it to him, and he thought that would help him for his sentencing court date. After the thirty days I never saw him again. Moral of the story: You cannot stop being a compulsive gambler for anyone else but yourself. I threw away a twenty-one-year marriage because my focus was to stop for somebody other than myself. It does not work. At some point you must be able to look at yourself in the mirror and recognize you are worth it, that you deserve a better life, a life without gambling.

There is no way to make a compulsive gambler a normal gambler. That is not possible. The disease is too strong. So many new compulsive gamblers come to GA to learn how to control their gambling. They really don't want to stop; they just want to learn ways to control it. Control is one of the biggest motivators to keep a compulsive gambler gambling like a madman. I gambled for at least two decades with the firm belief that I was in control of what I was doing. There are so many people I know in the program and that are new to the program that so want to be able to control their gambling in order that they may continue gambling without destroying themselves. I would always speak to how I viewed myself in full control of my actions and that I was doing what I wanted to do. Yeah, I wanted to gamble until my last dime was gone. Yeah, I wanted to take out the maximum daily amount off my debit card and lose it before going home. Yeah, I wanted to destroy my marriage. Yeah, I wanted to take my kids' money so they would have college debt to pay back when I could have and should have been able to pay their way through college. What a crock of crap. All this shows is that I was not in any type of control. In fact, the devil had me with this disease and I was nothing more than a worthless pawn.

For family members and loved ones of people with addictions, I can tell you as an addict that the last thing we would ever want to do is hurt any of you. We were fine with hurting ourselves because we have no self worth when we are in our addiction. We know what we are doing is wrong, yet our disease can take us away from sanity and convince us that we are going to right everything with a big win and we honestly believe it.

I think one of the most difficult things to do to get into the right state of mind for recovery is to slow down. When you are gambling and, in your addiction, there is no way you can do the crazy things you do at a slow pace. Your disease needs you to think and react to things at a frenetic pace to get you to do all the crazy and destructive things like I would do to myself. You must change the way you do things. You must change the way you think. Many people come to GA looking for a safer replacement to gambling. They come looking for the same high but minus the money losses and the destruction caused to caring loved ones. Unfortunately, there is no silver bullet to ward off compulsive gambling. To recover you must change. You must think slower. You must live slower, and while doing all of that you have to learn to relish the slowness that recovery provides. Yes, that was a correct statement. You must learn to relish and rejoice in the slowness of recovery. It feels different because it is fundamentally different. When I gambled I did so like a madman with very little thought to time or consequences. In recovery one thing you definitely have is time, so why not learn to welcome and relish all that time: a healthy time. A time where you are not hurting yourself or a loved one, and a time where you know what you are doing is the right thing to do.

I can remember early on in my recovery, the slowness of recovery. In the beginning I really had difficulty slowing down. My mind and my wants were always haunting me at a frenetic pace. I can remember dreaming a couple of times early on in my recovery that I was gambling, and the dream seemed so real that I would wake up sweating from nervousness, and shaky from believing that I did gamble again. I cannot remember ever being so scared before by a dream that I had. It took me at least three to six months of recovery for me to begin settling my mind and body while becoming used to the snail-like speed of recovery. I can remember laying out in the sun in the summertime and just lying and relaxing after a couple hours of sleep after work. I would lay back and just think. I would take in the day and focus on not gambling today. As the days passed, I became more confident that I could remain successful not gambling by continuing to do things differently in recovery than what I did when I gambled.

CHAPTER 8

PRISON, INSANITY OR DEATH

As I'm over halfway through writing my book, I strongly feel the need to dedicate a chapter solely to the term prison, insanity, or death. So here goes. Back on March 3, 2011, for me that possible outcome was oh so real and it didn't have to be. First, when you're at the point in your life where prison, insanity or death are your perceived best potential outcomes, you know that something with you internally is very wrong. No one wants to grow up and be a compulsive gambler or an addict of any type. It just happens. It does take time for the addiction to take hold but once it does, you learn it is much easier to become addicted than it is to become clean again, to become right-minded once again, to get back to being the person you believe you are. Even when in your addiction, you believe that you are taking the proper steps to rid yourself eventually from that addiction.

My belief was that if I was caught embezzling funds, then that would be the bottom that would get me to stop. Even though when that occurred and so far, I have stopped gambling, I can tell you in all honesty that was nothing but the wishful thinking my disease provided for me to gamble more. I truly believe my disease wanted my end game to be my killing myself and then somehow my disease would feel as if it had won. I think it wants that for most people who are addicted. All your disease needs to get you there is time. The mental disease of addiction is patient, while you the addict is anything but patient. Again, I do understand that I am talking about me and the way my mind works.

Remember the commercial, "This is your brain on drugs," and you were shown an egg frying in a pan. To me prison, insanity or death is even more important for everyone to hear; fellow addicts, loved ones of addicts, kids and schools. Yes, schools and here is why I say that. First off, life is about making choices. Every day you are making choices. The better choices you make, the easier and better your life is. It's that plain and simple; maybe too simple. My eldest son and daughter-in-law daily highlight the importance of making good choices with their children. My daughter does the same with my grandson. When I was a child, I never heard the term of making good choices. Not from my parents, grandparents, family, friends, enemies nor from my disease. Now I don't blame anybody for not hearing this when I was growing up, but what reason is there not to hear it now? Every week you hear about the Opioid Epidemic. Back when I grew up, we had the War on Drugs. Where is the preventative dialogue? Where is the preventative teaching? Like anything else, major issues occur when they go unnoticed for decades by those elected by us to prevent such catastrophes. This is nothing more than my opinion, but why do we not teach good choices or decision making in our schools? You could clearly show a developing child and teenager the benefits of making good choices and the positive impact they would have on their life versus the negative consequences of bad choices and the impact from those upon their lives. I get riled internally just writing my opinions on this matter.

There has been a tremendous impact over the past twenty years on our prison systems that are riddled with addicts. Again, to me many of them are good people with an addiction. Is a prison the proper place for people with an addiction? Unfortunately, right now it's the only place, unless you have lots of money to repeatedly go to rehabilitation before you commit a crime to fund your addiction. Once the money for rehab runs dry, then what do you have? Where do you go then? I was told if I had a drug or alcohol problem I could be sent to rehab on the state's dime. I told my probation officer, "No, I'm just a compulsive gambler." Then the crickets in the room took over.

When I was a child my step-grandfather was housed in Manteno State Hospital, Illinois for several years after physically assaulting my grandmother and it was referred to as a mental hospital. Back then mental hospitals were not well revered, and I don't know enough about it to speak intelligently. But doesn't it make sense to place people with an addiction or mental illness within a rehab facility for the addict and a mental institution for the mentally ill, rather than incarcerating them in a prison? Like that is going to rehabilitate and teach them not to be an addict. It's silly that in this day and age when we know so much about everything else, that we do not know more about addiction and offer more treatments to extinguish these diseases. Instead, we place these people in prison, buy large quantities of overdose drugs for law enforcement, hospitals, and ambulances, and then let these addicted people get back to their normal lives of addiction. All of this makes me very sad and irritated.

Moving on to insanity, I have no issues in clearly communicating that I was insane in my disease of gambling. My actions and behavior were totally inconsistent with my behavior now that I am in recovery and not gambling. It still amazes me that I could behave so insanely for such a long period of time while at every point of my life while an addict, be firmly convinced that my decision making was well thought out and solid. With recovery comes clarity, actual clarity not the kind of clarity I thought I had before when I gambled. It's funny how your mind plays with you in an addiction. You know you're not doing the right thing, but when gambling I tended to never think about that. Now I know most compulsive gamblers don't look at prison, insanity, or death the way I do. If you have never been at that crossroad, you also believe you will never be at that crossroad. Unfortunately, that thought process would be inaccurate. All you need is time, and the progressive nature of the disease will take care of the rest to bring you to the same crossroad where I was.

Death is the end of the line for the addiction. Only the addiction wins at this point. The addict loses and the loved ones of the addict live with the reality of their loved one's disease for the rest of their lives. So many people in this country are addicts of some type, but even more impacted are the loved ones. I truly believe prison or death are unnecessary for any problem gambler. Yet I also understand and respect how easy it is for a compulsive gambler to attain either one based upon the lifestyle of the addiction, coupled with the enormous mental anguish the addicted person lives with on a continual basis. That's another reason why recovery is so important. You can go back to leading a normal and productive life, but honestly it takes a lot of work and God's mercy.

CHAPTER 9

GAMBLERS ANONYMOUS

Gamblers Anonymous is a special place. I believe for a compulsive gambler who truly wants to change their life and stop gambling, it is the only choice. I often talk in GA when a new person arrives, how vital it is to continue attending GA meetings as they try to recover from their insidious disease. The fact is there are no other options, at least no other options that worked for me. I can remember going to my first GA meeting over fifteen years ago, primarily to appease my wife at the time, and to try and slow down on the gambling craziness that my life had become by learning how to better control my weakness. At the time that is how I viewed my problem, not as an addiction, not as a disease. I was simply a weak person. The thought of that being true kept me gambling for decades. I kept trying to prove myself wrong by getting that big win that would allow me to stop gambling and make up for all the wrong I had done. Sadly, no matter how much I would win, I would gamble it back and lose more.

In GA I've heard people talk of needing to know why they gambled and the need to talk to a professional about their gambling. One thing I came to believe in GA is that no one understands the behavior and thought process like another compulsive gambler. You would think understanding this would be natural, but that's not how a compulsive gambler thinks. I walked into my first meeting and came out shocked afterward. I couldn't believe other people thought as screwed up as I did. I was truly amazed. At GA you find truly decent, respectable people with a nasty disease.

We read the little yellow book which I personally highly recommend as required first year reading for all problem gamblers. This yellow book was me. It speaks to the dream world of the problem gambler and that entire paragraph was me to a tee.

I can remember during my first year of recovery my second time around in GA feeling like Darth Vader while listening to certain people speak, even some with some clean time. I could feel the disease speaking within them. I could hear and feel how badly they wanted to gamble again, and recovery for them would become more of a challenge. Throughout that first year I felt it was important for me to alter the way I think. If I was going to think like others I would listen to, then no doubt I would gamble again. Mind you, the people speaking did not believe they were saying anything wrong or that they were headed back to gamble some more, but I'm telling you I could feel their disease within them taking back control just by what they said and, more importantly, how they said it. What I try to get new members to understand is that this is a disease. I tell them my story of how my doctor of ten years ran out his office door when I told him I was a compulsive gambler. He sent in the nurse to give me a piece of paper to see a psychologist.

I went to see the psychologist for about three weeks. After that amount of time, I realized that there was no magic pill for him to give me that would curb my addiction. I also realized that neither one of us truly understood the other.

As concerns other people who had to know the reason why they gamble and sought the help of a professional counselor, after years of treatment I have still not seen one remain in recovery for over five years. I don't mean to disrespect people that feel that is important to stopping, but I have just never seen a compulsive gambler stop gambling by doing so. I'm sure there are people out there that have, but like I say, I have never seen those people at a GA meeting.

My second time around in GA was when I was at my lowest point in my gambling life. In my second meeting Jim A. uttered those infamous words of prison, insanity, or death. I believe over seventy-five percent of the newcomers in that room do not take in or believe that statement. That's not going to happen to me. I am above that. I am better than that. Stinky thinking at its finest. For me, however, I was engulfed with those words. Thank God for Jim A. What a blessing. He told me something I absolutely needed to hear and will never forget for the rest of my life. He will never know how his words have assisted me as I walk through my new life, unless he buys this book of course. Prison, insanity, or death. If you continue to gamble you can look forward to any or all three. When you really think about it, who on God's green earth finds any one of those outcomes as potentially satisfactory. My heart bleeds with the number of compulsive gamblers who take their own life every day of every year. Some never even make it to GA to even give the program a chance. That's a significant indication how difficult it is to live with this disease. As a compulsive gambler when you read of someone's suicide, you never read that it was because they were a compulsive gambler. Never and that is a shame. As compulsive gamblers we are the uncounted. You will see on television where they give you an eight hundred number to call, yet many calls to the eight hundred number given are not even answered. There is no news or reporting on any of this. I think this is one of the reasons compulsive gamblers feel so low about themselves. Even though so many of us exist, no one talks out loud about us. States continue to bring in more casinos, and Indian tribes and corporations continue to create new compulsive gamblers every day and no one cares. No one reports about any potential negative effects on the surrounding community or its people. It's all about the money. Greed from the corporation side and the necessity for states to find greater revenue streams while, in turn, destroying the lives of problem gamblers as well as those of their families. Gambling is everywhere today. We have people that come in hooked on the daily lottery and scratch off tickets. These tickets are available virtually everywhere. Go to get gas and what do you walk into in the front at every register? Gambling.

I can remember my first meeting with my probation officer. He asked me if I was addicted to drugs or alcohol. I said I was a compulsive gambler and that was my only addiction. He told me too bad because if I was addicted to drugs or alcohol, they would send me to rehab. That statement kind of blew me away. He did say I would have to attend GA meetings and it was on all the paperwork. Yet, even though I reported to a probation officer for four years until my restitution was paid, not once did they ask me if I attended a GA meeting. Their primary concern was that I was working and that my monthly payments were paid on time. If I was in arrears, they would not allow me to travel out of state to visit my daughter and grandson. So, money was both their and my major concern.

After three years, upon my request to the probation officer to release me from probation based upon my payment history and less than five thousand dollars remaining to be paid, my probation officer made this request to the judge.

The judge said no, that I would have to pay the restitution off in full before he would release me from probation. He was a man of his word. Once I paid off my restitution, within a week my probation was removed, and I received my probation release papers. Once paid the release was given.

I was thankful to have that part of my new life over with. The only reason I mention it is that there is absolutely nothing the court system or our government provides to a compulsive gambler or their family members who are adversely affected. Yet our government helps anybody and everybody except for us. It seems to me that all we have as compulsive gamblers is GA and thank God for it. Unfortunately, there is nothing else, no magic pill or treatment. It is obvious few dollars go into researching this disease. I believe that is wrong. This sentiment of mine includes all addictions. The only difference between an alcoholic, drug user and compulsive gambler is our drug of choice. The internal and external pain we cause is consistent for us all with any loved ones we touch. What a shame. This reality makes me very sad. I don't believe anyone is placing the necessary focus to combat the addictions that exist within our society.

Concerning GA, let me say first off, I love GA and the people within it. In my opinion, these are some of the finest people I have met, as well of some of the most ill. When GA came into existence at a chance meeting in California back in 1957, the attendees were recovered alcoholics who became compulsive gamblers and AA meetings did not assist them in stopping gambling. My only issue with GA is that it is meant to be nonpublic, nonpolitical, and not to be spoken of or about to any news agencies. For over sixty years this is what GA has done, meeting in churches or wherever an organization will rent a room at a reduced price so fellow problem gamblers can come together and meet. Unfortunately, in 1957 there were no off-track betting facilities, no state sponsored lottery tickets, no federal sponsored lottery tickets, no casinos located in over thirty plus states, no pull tabs, jai alai, and no online gambling or any type of gambling you could possibly imagine. The reason I'm saying this is because I know how difficult it is to step inside that GA room for the first time. We know as compulsive gamblers that there are thousands to millions of us with the disease that will not be able to accept the fact that they have a problem, and that GA can assist them in recovering from the disease. In my experience many who come to GA simply want to learn how to control their gambling rather than stopping gambling. It's very sad when you are sitting in a room every week with anywhere from five to twenty-five participants and you know there are so many others out there suffering, so many that will be leaving the casino or racetrack and looking for the right tree along the highway to take away all this pain and suffering. Yet even though you are at such a low to even consider running into a tree to end the cycle of pain, less than twenty-four hours later all thought of that has been erased from your mind and off you go again trying to win back all you have lost over and over again.

Educated people know we compulsive gamblers exist, yet we are part of little conversation designed to assist us. The truly diabolical fact is that I have seen that the elderly are often most adversely affected. With the advent of casinos everywhere, compulsive gambling retirees on limited incomes are taken advantage of by gambling providers as they drain their bank accounts until empty, and then they are tossed aside to their family members to take care of and worry about. I have repeatedly seen family members take over the role of parent and the elderly parent become the child, resulting in torturous wounds created within the relationship of the family members of the diseased parent. Compulsive gambling is seldom viewed by the people without the disease, as a disease. I am convinced that it is, and I will go to my grave believing so. People view a compulsive gambler as someone who is weak, a liar and selfish. All of which is true, but it is because of the active disease within them.

When I was active in my compulsive gambling, I lied all the time. For some reason it was easier for me to lie than to tell the truth. That is the disease within. After being clean for over a year I noticed certain character changes within myself. I significantly reduced my level of lies down to not being able to remember a recent lie of any kind. When I gambled, I knew I was lying ninety-seven percent of the time. As a compulsive gambler I felt I was a very weak person, even though I didn't want anyone to realize this in me. That feeling of weakness kept me gambling for decades. Chasing my losses and considering myself a loser for my bad choices are all part of the disease. This disease wants to create a life of chaos for you. It does not want you to slowly consider anything.

Thank God for GA and its members, but I think it's time for GA 2025, a futuristic updating of the program to service more members into the next century, as well as attract more new members who need the assistance. Also, this new program would require working closely with gaming corporations and local, state, and federal agencies in government to financially assist with research for disease prevention, and treatments for those in need. We cannot in good conscience allow what is happening daily to compulsive gamblers active in their disease without trying to stop it. People taking their own lives on a daily basis for unknown reasons should not be acceptable within our society. The only people that truly know the reasoning are the loved ones left behind to live with the memory.

Many educated people do not believe compulsive gambling is a disease. I do and will until I die. I find it extremely helpful in my recovery to view it as such. I believe I take my affliction more seriously by considering it a disease. At GA I often refer to my medicine or pill that I take to treat this insidious disease is going to GA. I know that a compulsive gambler has no real chance to stop gambling for any prolonged period of time without being a part of the GA family. I know and am comfortable with the fact that I will have to go to GA meetings for the rest of my life. Now that belief might get you somewhat ridiculed at a meeting by another GA member with a long period of recovery, and they would be right to a point. The success of a person's recovery depends upon them living and focusing on their disease, and not gambling one day at a time. However, for me I revel in the fact that I will be an active GA member until the day that I die. The idea of dying while in recovery and not being active in my gambling disease I view as an absolute blessing. For decades I was so fearful that I would die active in my disease. The thought of that really affected me. I so wanted that not to be the case, but when you gamble for as long as I did, hopelessness is a reality. Thank God and GA for taking away the hopelessness I had felt for so long and for instilling such faith and blessings into my new life. What a monumental difference it is to be sober and thankful for life, rather than simply existing in it.

CHAPTER 10

THE IMPORTANCE OF STEP ONE OF THE TWELVE STEPS

Step One is one of the most important steps in recovery. It states, "We admitted we were powerless over gambling – that our lives had become unmanageable." Many people think Step One shows weakness, the same as stepping into a GA meeting for the first time; the weakness that we are unable to control or resolve the issue of compulsive gambling. In our mind when we are gambling, we believe that we are in full control and all powerful. The high of the disease makes you believe you are invulnerable, that you will surely win. The only question is how much. Giving up control and admitting weakness are incomprehensible for a compulsive gambler to even consider when in gambling mode. My first time in GA, I was clean for twelve and a half months. This was around fifteen years ago. Every week for twelve and a half months, I would read or say Step One at least once each meeting. I could read it just fine. The only issue I had was truly understanding what it meant and how it could assist me in stopping gambling in following it. So many people come to GA meetings without ever taking in the true meaning of Step One. So many that come in want to learn how to control their problem, rather than eliminating and resolving it. Like me they breeze through the reading without focusing on its true meaning and how to use it. It wasn't until about a year's worth of clean time in early 2012, that I finally began to buy in and understand what I believed to be the true meaning of Step One and how I could use it to assist me with not gambling again. What follows is my attempt at trying to explain my understanding of Step One.

Admitting I was powerless became a feeling that I welcomed over time. Recognizing that when I gambled was when I was truly powerless was the exact opposite of how I viewed it when I gambled. That is one of the blessings of recovery. Your thought process takes a 180-degree turn in what you believed in pre- and post-gambling. In recovery you know that your thoughts and current beliefs are the correct ones. Those thoughts and beliefs back when I gambled were nothing but bullshit, even though I was convinced that it was true for decades. I needed to learn that with powerlessness came strength and control, two things I didn't have much of when I was gambling. If you can truly believe that you're powerless to this disease, to me that is the beginning for fighting it, hence Step One. When you admit to being powerless over gambling, there is a certain freedom to buying into that statement. I am not in control, and I don't want to be in control. This is how I think in recovery. I can tell you for a fact that I never thought that way when I gambled.

I like to say in GA that control is vastly overrated. As it pertains to a compulsive gambler, it is a necessity. How could one gamble thousands to millions of dollars over a lifetime and genuinely do it with the belief that he or she has no control over it. When you hear someone in a GA meeting speak to the need of learning to control their gambling or attaining control over it, you can rest assured that person will gamble again because they have not bought into Step One. If you are trying to control something, the last thing you would recognize is that you are powerless to control this disease. It doesn't mean you're weak, it simply means you are diseased. Your mind is affected by the disease of compulsive gambling, and it inhibits you from a rational thought process. This is because the disease wants you to gamble. It wants to convince you to ride the roller coaster as long as you can possibly tolerate, and when it realizes you are done, then all it wants you to do is simply end your life and it will be on to the next compulsive gambling diseased individual. What a shame, a once bright and shiny life taken by this awful disease. Family members left with the remains of the destruction, questioning, wondering, while never knowing or truly understanding why. Today this occurs daily, leaving family members shattered in many cases.

You could say a compulsive gambler is weak, selfish, egotistical, and reckless, all of which would be true. But if you could look at compulsive gambling like people look at cancer, maybe you will understand it differently. Here's what I mean. In compulsive gambling weakness, control issues, lying, egotistical, and recklessness are only a few of the symptoms of this disease. Take away this disease from the individual and these symptoms as well as many others that come with this disease are gone. No longer is the recovering compulsive gambler weak or a chronic liar, egotistical, or reckless in their behavior. Those negative behaviors go away when the disease is in remission and the person is in recovery.

Mention a disease and nine times out of ten, people will have empathy for the individual or family impacted by the disease. When it comes to a compulsive gambler, an alcoholic, a heroin addict, a meth addict, and a sex addict, nine out of ten people will have little to no empathy for those individuals. They consider these addicts weak and that they had the effects of the addiction coming to them. The nonaddict does not understand the disease of addiction. Honestly, I don't think they ever will because they are not wired mentally like we are, thankfully.

Step One also states, "that our lives had become unmanageable." Truer words were never spoken. You talk about unmanageable; every compulsive gambler knows this side of it. It causes you to lie about everything, even when you don't need to. It causes you to run to the mailbox before your husband or wife can get to the mail. You certainly don't want them figuring out what you have been up to with the finances related to your gambling. The unmanageability of the disease is probably the single biggest factor of recruitment in GA.

As a compulsive gambler, when you are at your wits end with the disease and in dire straits, the unmanageability of the disease I believe causes us to take our first steps into the GA program. Keeping you in the program requires a lot more effort and realization on the compulsive gambler's part, because the disease wants none of that. It simply wants you to get back to unmanageability land. This is where working the twelve steps is vital to a lasting and continued recovery for most problem gamblers. The steps are in order for a reason. To succeed in recovery, you can't begin working the steps with Step Four. You must start with Step One, and you must be successful in working Step One to achieve a lasting recovery, in my opinion. That is why I believe Step One is so vital to a person's recovery. Learn to embrace that, "We admitted we were powerless over gambling – that our lives had become unmanageable" theme song. Be proud to have finally recognized that you were powerless over your gambling and that gambling has caused so many problems for you in your life. Don't be sad or feel ashamed because this is a disease of the mind. Be thankful that you finally have recognized that and bought into the words of Step One. Thank God for helping me to finally see this as a disease, and with that I take it as seriously as I would any disease of which I would become afflicted. One way I consistently refer back to Step One is that anytime I get serious thoughts of gambling again, I review Step One. That reinforces the belief in me that I am powerless over my disease and that's why I cannot gamble. Rather than viewing that as a weakness, I now view that reality as a strength. I play the scenario through now in my mind rather than at a racetrack or casino. When I run it through my mind, I know how the scenario will always end if I ever do decide to go back to gambling again. Step One keeps me safe and prevents me from doing that. The reality of Step One scared me when I gambled, whereas now I am blessed by it. I truly don't know how anyone could gamble again if they simply replayed Step One prior to gambling. I do know though that to achieve a successful recovery, there is more to achieving it than simply Step One. Steps Two and Three are just as vital as Step One is to achieve a lasting sobriety.

CHAPTER 11

THE NECESSITY OF STEPS TWO & THREE OF THE TWELVE STEPS

Steps Two and Three refer to belief in a higher power and to me, that is God. Step Two is "Came to believe that a power greater than ourselves could restore us to a normal way of thinking and living." Step Three is "Made a decision to turn our will and our lives over to the care of this power of our own understanding." For Step Two, many compulsive gamblers come to GA without a higher power. Many view GA as their higher power, especially early on in their recovery. I was like that. Even though I believed in God, my entire thought process around God and my life revolved around lots of stinky thinking. I had trouble believing God wanted the best for me based upon all my gambling sins. I felt, to a large degree, that I deserved the problems that I created through my gambling.

Many times during my first year of recovery, as I would speak and tell my story at GA, I would often refer to myself and my life as a compulsive gambler of forty-four years as a bad reality show that God loved to watch. Each week a new problem and, for the final decade, a new low time after time. I was very angry. That anger allowed me to gamble for decades. Deep down I felt God had forsaken me, that he enjoyed watching me struggle throughout those forty-four years of nonstop gambling. I could not understand how he would allow my life to spiral down to the point that it had or allow me to live such a roller coaster type of life with various highs coupled with tremendous lows. I would hear people with lots of clean time speak each week about God as their higher power. For the first year of my recovery, that tended to go in one ear and out the other.

After around fifteen months of clean time, I began to feel a change in my beliefs and thought process, like the fog that I'd been living under throughout my life was finally beginning to dissipate and that I was beginning to see things clearly for the first time in a long, long time. I noticed certain occurrences in my life that began to make me recognize that God was in my life and guiding me through my own recovery. When I would get down or stinky thinking would creep back into my mind, God would assist me by putting me in positions and places where I would receive a clear message to stay the course, and things would get better if I only did not gamble today and continued to move forward every day in that manner. Multiple things were happening around me almost daily. Frankly, I have a feeling similar instances were occurring when I was in my disease, but I was so focused on my addiction that I never even noticed. I truthfully believe God had made numerous attempts to put people in my life and to put me in places to assist me in stopping gambling throughout my life. Unfortunately, being as strong as I was in my disease, I was unable to witness or comprehend any of these attempts by God for my attention. Here are some examples of what I mean.

My first year of recovery, I ate for basically $3.70 each day. I know what you're thinking; that's impossible but it's not. I was working overnight as a stocker at Walmart during my first year of recovery from 10 p.m. to 7 a.m., five days a week. So, during the day I would get home, fall asleep for a couple of hours, and then go to Sam's Club for lunch which consisted of a Pizza Combo (a slice of pizza and a Diet Coke) virtually six out of seven days a week. During work we would have break time from 2 a.m. to 3 a.m. When I didn't have a car, I would buy a Lunchable for $1.06 at the store. When I was able to buy a car eight months later, I would drive to McDonalds and order a McDouble for $1.06. What a treat the McDouble was over the Lunchable. I was so thankful to be able to eat that on each overnight I worked. Mind you, when I gambled, I would never order a McDouble, nor believe it to be any type of a treat. Somehow, little things began to mean something in my life. When I gambled, I would consider what I was doing as slumming, just a terrible way of thinking. So many people live without basic necessities while others take for granted all that they have. I find that whole situation sad, but very true.

At Walmart, my job as a stocker was much more physical than my prior managerial roles, even though I always considered myself a hard worker. I ended up becoming the chemical aisle and paper aisle stocker on a nightly basis. I quickly learned why no one else was stocking chemicals or wanting to stock them. It would usually take me four to five hours to stock all the chemical aisles all night. In the beginning it would take me all night to complete. I can tell you though, whoever stocks the chemical aisle at a Walmart or similar business works their behind off. The constant chemical odor over the entire evening initially can be nauseating. In time somehow you become used to it. The heavy lifting also challenges you. I quickly learned why no one liked to do it which is why I was doing it, being simply thankful at this point that I had a job so I could make enough money to live. As difficult as the work and lifestyle was for me throughout my first year of recovery, I was blessed to have lost over fifty pounds. I went from two hundred thirty pounds to a low of one hundred seventy-five pounds. I didn't mention that I was also going to BioLife and donating plasma for money twice a week. After losing over fifty pounds, I felt that I was back in a condition at almost age fifty that I hadn't been in since I was in my thirties. I felt great, strong, and fit. What a blessing! God brought me back in shape. From being overweight, tired, and lethargic, God got me back to my feel-good weight. There's no doubt that this experience has increased my life expectancy from where it was when I gambled.

During my second year of recovery, I changed jobs by getting fired from Walmart for taking four P&G Brand Saver coupon books out of the Sunday paper, placing them in another paper and paying for only two of the papers. As I was exiting Walmart, I was stopped by a plain-clothed security officer and taken back to a side room. They asked me what I did, and I told them exactly what I did. I told them I didn't realize there was anything wrong with what I did, and I would pay the additional three dollars. They would have none of it. They said I stole six dollars worth of books from four papers. I told them that I did not take the paper, only the P&G Brandsaver monthly coupon book. To make a long story short, five days later I was fired for the incident. I paid six dollars to Walmart to pay off the debt and then I had to notify my probation officer of what I did and what happened because of it. I lied to my mother and my children about why I was fired. I told them that Walmart learned I was a convicted felon and they had to fire me. That is one of the few times that I had lied during my recovery. I felt bad but more importantly, I really felt stupid. I couldn't believe that I thought taking those extra coupon books was okay. My probation officer was simply concerned that I would get another job, so I could continue to stay on track with making my monthly restitution payments.

Suddenly it hit me that I was out of work again and that I would have to go out and pound the pavement to try and obtain another minimum wage job. I was so nervous, so scared. Only a convicted felon knows how difficult it is to simply go out and fill out an application. Most people don't think twice to complete an employment application. As a convicted felon, I found it very nerve-racking, painful, and almost debilitating. I kept thinking how I should fill it out, meaning do I check yes or no as a convicted felon. Many employers won't tell you, but when you check yes, they move onto the next candidate and file yours in the garbage. I worked for multiple companies when I was in management and that is what we did. As I went online and physically to several establishments to fill out applications, there was one major difference I noticed in me this second time around of job seeking, as I was completing the applications. The difference was that I answered all the questions honestly. I put my felony information down on every application that asked. To me that was amazing.

I filled out an online application for a Pizza Hut delivery driver job where it asked the question if I had a felony within the past twelve months and I answered no, as it had been fifteen months. I'm at my Friday night GA meeting and about ten minutes into the meeting I received a local call on my cell phone, and they left a message. I went to the restroom, called my voicemail, and learned that Pizza Hut called to set up an interview with me. I called them from the restroom and set up an interview for Monday. I go to the interview on Monday and thankfully, all went well. They would check my driving record and God knows what else and get back to me. Four days later they called me to come in and begin training. Mind you, for the first couple of weeks I wasn't even sure that I was hired, even though I was working there. I didn't know how long it took to obtain the driver's license information and if I would be approved or not. My driving record was fine. I just didn't know if my arrest warrant from over fifteen months ago was still on my driving record. What a terrible, helpless feeling.

I started at Pizza Hut the following week and the first week consisted of computer training modules and shadowing another driver. Finally, by my second week I am driving and making money. I was so thankful to have a job, so thankful to have money starting to come in again. Throughout my first two years at Pizza Hut, I found myself consistently scared that at some point I would lose my existing job based upon my sins of the past and the felony that was on my record. I was constantly fearful I would lose my job.

I told you about my grandson, Ben, and the effect that he had on my recovery in year two, and with the addition of my new job things could not have worked out better for me in improving my quality of life. I was working until one or two a.m. and then sleeping until eight a.m. to begin watching Ben while my daughter Nikki went to work. I was rested and I felt so much better while watching Ben. Early on, I was making more money at Pizza Hut than what I was earning at Walmart. As time went on and I became better at learning the delivery area which allowed me to take more deliveries and earn more money, my income doubled and then eventually tripled what I was making at Walmart. There is no doubt in my mind that God positioned me at Walmart for the amount of time that He did, and then moved me and my life forward when I went to Pizza Hut. By then I was in recovery, not gambling, making decent money, and paying down my restitution like never before. What a blessing and when you consider how it all occurred, it was absolutely amazing. Thank God.

As a delivery driver you have good days and you have bad days, sometimes really bad days. Bad days usually consist of delivering pizza, pasta and wings to people who do not tip you. Mind you, there would be no pizza delivery drivers if no one tipped, as a driver could not make enough money to live on. I can remember one night I was having an awful day and I cried out to God after delivering to another person who did not tip. I asked God for strength and questioned how people in good conscience could not tip for service, especially from someone driving it to them and carrying it up three flights of stairs or a mile to their hotel room. As I was at this low point, my next delivery was to a mom and her daughter at a rehabilitation center. I have delivered to them before. I deliver their food, the daughter takes the food from me as the mom, in her wheelchair, in pain and moving slowly, smiles and signs the credit card receipt while giving me a five-dollar tip. I walk to my car in tears as I look up into the sky, get in my car and start bawling like a baby. In my mind I am thanking God for all that he has provided me and questioning how I can be such an ass. Here is this woman around my age who appeared to have been in some sort of accident requiring rehabilitation, sharing dinner with her daughter who I am sure was totally focused on her mom's health, and I walk in the door all down and depressed because my last five deliveries did not provide me with a tip. You can call all these situations I name in this chapter coincidence, but at that exact moment I finally got and received it. It was not coincidence. None of it had been. This was divine intervention. This was God guiding me, showing me the way, and for once I was listening and following. I was a true believer.

I have stated that I believed in God prior to my recovery, but the way I believed was frankly wrong. I would thank God when I would hit it big gambling, but I would also ask why he had forsaken me when I would lose consistently. In my old life where realistically I had so much to be thankful for, I was thankful for very little. The only times I can remember being thankful during my first life was when my children were born, and they were born healthy. Now I am thankful for so much more: my kids, my grandkids, Julie, Julie's family, GA, recovery, my friends, vacation, my job, my life, and the absolute beauty life has to offer to those that can see it, those who are not addicted.

I have not seen a lasting recovery for a compulsive gambler who does not have Steps Two and Three down. Many fake it until they make it by using GA as their higher power, but personally I don't believe GA alone can provide a compulsive gambler with long term recovery without God in their lives. God has convinced me that he wants nothing but the best for me, but to achieve the best for me I must do my part and I am good with that.

I listen to Joel Osteen a lot now as I have Sirius XM while I'm working and driving, and I enjoy listening to his messages daily. I find him very positive and uplifting. When I gambled, I lived a negative life. I focused on the negative incessantly. Now I try to focus on the positive because there is so much of it. My thought process has done a total 180-degree turn compared to how I thought when I was gambling. I am so thankful for that. I am now receptive to God and even God's messengers. I continue to learn how to live and improve my new life through these methods.

I speak with Julie regularly that I have God's favor. I continue to work on her belief system as well that she has it also. I believe I've told you before how great of a woman Julie is, but like me Julie has never fully realized or fully recognized the favor God has shined on us throughout our lives. We were both focused on our struggles, rather than the beauty of the journey of our lives. Prior to meeting me Julie was married for thirty-one years to an outstanding man, husband, father, and grandfather; a hardworking, family-oriented man who passed away way too young at fifty-one years old from colon cancer. They had two beautiful girls and now have four beautiful grandchildren. I have a very good relationship with my ex-wife of twenty-one years, three awesome kids and four beautiful grandchildren. As hard as times could be, there were so many times in our lives that were beautiful, taking us to where we are now. Thankfully, I can now see the beauty in my life, respect it and appreciate it.

Thank you to Joel Osteen for his positive messages. I do believe that he means what he says. It's so easy to be in a good place and then for life's reasons and events, to temporarily forget all of that. Joel's messages always assist me with removing stinky thinking when it enters my mind. For my recovery I have come to appreciate listening to a couple of his messages on a daily basis. They're always positive, well meaning and well balanced. Understanding that to get to where God wants you to be, your journey up to that point was necessary. That's a difficult one for a compulsive gambler to believe at first because it's so hard to come to terms with after all the years of crazy gambling, crazy behavior, and the ups and despicable downs of this disease, that this was a necessary part of our lives. The pain we have caused ourselves and our friends and loved ones is really a difficult feeling with which to come to terms. But to achieve a full, healthy recovery, you must come to terms with the fact that when you were under the control of this disease, you did a lot of bad things to yourself and others that you would never do if your disease was in remission, and you were not acting on it.

For me, once I had Steps One, Two and Three down, I felt a rush of comfort run through my very being, a rush that made me confident like never before that I could fight my disease and win. This feeling only came about when I had wholeheartedly bought into Steps One through Three. I truly believed that I was powerless over my gambling, that I would never achieve control of it. Again, control issues are bad. You need to lose the thought process that you need to be in control. Turn the control over to God rather than taking on all that responsibility on your own. That move alone provided me with so much peace and comfort. All the years I had spent trying to control everyone else and myself were a futile mess. The craziest thing was that my belief when I chose to gamble was that was when I was in the most control of my life. What a crock! Stinky thinking at it's finest. No longer do I have to look back in bitter disappointment for the road up to March 3, 2011, where my life had taken me. I could find a place of comfort and happiness to where I am at today, with hope and purpose reinvigorated within my soul. Such a different belief and feeling than when I was gambling.

CHAPTER 12

WORKING STEPS FOUR THROUGH TWELVE

Once you have Steps One through Three down, you are ready to move forward with Step Four. Again, I believe the steps are in numerical order for a reason. I also think it's important to work the steps after at least one year of clean time. I say this because very few compulsive gamblers who come into GA have Steps One through Three completed. In fact, I believe those three steps are the most critical for long-term success in stopping gambling. It should be no surprise that these steps will take the longest to fully understand and commit to. In the beginning a new GA member has so much going on in their lives and in their mind that fully comprehending the meaning of the steps and working them properly is virtually impossible early in their recovery. With bill collectors calling, spouses or loved ones ready to separate themselves from the compulsive gambler, it is very difficult for a compulsive gambler to be able to focus on working the steps when their most important task for each day is to simply not gamble today.

Those of you reading this who are not compulsive gamblers will never fully understand the difficulty that the compulsive gambler struggles with daily regarding the One Day at A Time statement and lifestyle. It sounds so easy to do when, in fact, it requires you to change your lifestyle and thought process that sometimes has been at your core, as in my case, for a lifetime. With all that said, recovery is still doable. I'm a prime example of that because after forty-four years of chronic, nonsensical gambling, I was able to put my disease in remission and live life in a One Day at A Time lifestyle and learn to relish it while doing it.

On to Step Four: "Made a Searching and Fearless Moral and Financial Inventory of Ourselves." The most important thing to be when working Step Four is honest. You must understand that the last thing a compulsive gambler exudes when gambling is honesty. Going through Step Four, you will get a sense of where you are in your recovery simply through your honesty. Here's what I mean. If you find that you are listing out every bad act you ever committed while gambling, that would be a good, honest start. However, if you find you are leaving out certain acts for whatever reason, then you are not completing Step Four as required for long-term success. This was especially true for me when I first attempted working the steps in Chicago ten years before my eventual gambling demise. I had a sponsor and listened to him and began working the steps. My mistake was that I was taking in very little. When I did Step Four the first time, I was not fully honest. I had left out certain bad acts for which I thought my sponsor might think less of me.

In 2012 when I completed Step Four, it was a totally different experience for me. First, I had Steps One through Three down the second time around, no baloney, and I truly believed in those steps. What I can't get over is how I thought I was working the steps the first time around, yet I had accomplished absolutely nothing in working and understanding them properly. The most important thing in working Step Four is to be honest and open to listing all your past mistakes that you can remember. You must remember that this is a disease, and that is why you did the dastardly things that you previously did. Don't hold back. Simply make sure your list is honest and complete. Once you've completed that task it's time to move on to Step Five. I will say that for me, once I completed Steps One through Three which took me a year and a half into my recovery, it only took me three months to complete Steps Four through Twelve.

For Step Five we "Admitted to Ourselves and To Another Human Being the Exact Nature of Our Wrongs." I think you will find it much easier to write down all your dastardly deeds versus telling each of them to someone else. I would highly recommend a sponsor for anyone looking to complete the twelve steps. Their assistance should be invaluable. In speaking about your previous indiscretions, you should welcome the opportunity to remove the guilt and baggage associated with your disease and recognizing this as your behavior of the past where you suffered for so long through this debilitating disease. It's important to be comfortable and have confidence in your sponsor because you will be telling him or her your deepest, darkest secrets; secrets so explosive in your heart and mind that you would never be able to tell your loved ones. There is most likely nothing you can say to him or her that they haven't done themselves or heard from someone else before. One area to be careful of is telling your sponsor what you think they want to hear, rather than truly communicating the exact nature of your wrongs. In feeling free by listing all of your issues, you can feel even more free from your disease by honestly communicating them to your sponsor. When you do this step correctly, it's amazing the amount of stress of which you can rid yourself. With Step Five honest openness and completeness are critical to performing it prior to moving on to Step Six.

Step Six speaks to the fact that we, "Were entirely ready to have these defects of character removed." When you really think about that statement, you realize how important, yet challenging this is for a compulsive gambler, but only for a recovering one. The reason I state it that way is that if a compulsive gambler reads that while actively gambling, the easy answer from him or her is no, meaning, "I am not entirely ready to change anything to do with my gambling, let alone being ready to have my character defects removed when I don't believe I have any." When you're gambling it's a total 180 in that you believe your actual defects are strengths. When you're in recovery, you clearly see that there were no strengths in your behavior when you gambled, only weaknesses that kept you stunted by your disease. Please note that when I get into talking about you or your behavior towards compulsive gambling, I am talking about my own. I do believe, however, that an extremely high percentage of compulsive gamblers would fall into this similar mindset of beliefs. Starting out in Step Six, you must make a list of your character defects. Again, the ability to be real and honest in your behavioral assessments is the key to successfully accomplishing Step Six.

Here is my list of character defects that I was entirely ready to have removed from me as I began to walk through recovery. First, let's start with anger. When I gambled, I loved anger. I would always look forward to an argument with my ex-wife that would quickly lead me to go out and gamble for the day, evening, or both. Anger was a necessary evil for me to gamble compulsively for over four decades of my life. I also harbored so much anger upon myself for the thoughtless things I had done over the course of my gambling life. I was angry at everybody, the guy who jumped in line in front of me keeping me from betting my winner, or the person at the casino hitting a jackpot on the slot machine that was mine and how dare he or she play on it, let alone win big in front of me when that winner should have been me. Same way on playing numbers on the roulette wheel and getting enough chips down to cover the numbers I wanted, and then realizing I left out one of my numbers and guess which number came up on the roulette wheel. What I've learned through recovery is that my anger caused me to continue to gamble uncontrollably for decades. Once you lessen the anger, you lessen the volume from the bad guy in your head who wants to destroy you.

Another character defect of mine I needed to work on in recovery was arrogance. When I gambled, I was oh so cocky about everything and everyone. I would toss ego in as well with my arrogance. This disease really feeds ego and arrogance into the compulsive gambler. Casinos have their tiered player levels, and everyone wants platinum level and to be considered a high roller, whether they are one or not. It's funny but in GA we talk about the different award levels we achieved through our gambling. Companies will provide different award levels to entice gamblers to continue to gamble. A compulsive gambler will gamble in excess to achieve higher award levels. During this it seems perfectly normal. When in recovery long enough, you recognize the insanity of chasing these award levels.

One of my favorite stories is from our Thursday night GA leader Mike, who has over fifteen years of clean time after decades of compulsive gambling. He talks about his free satin jacket the casino gave him for being a high roller. Then Mike talks about the $25,000 he lost that weekend to obtain the "free" jacket. His story provides an excellent peek into the blinders a compulsive gambler wears with his or her disease. Until recovery, Mike had always looked at that jacket with pride as having been provided to him free of charge for being such a high roller. Mike in recovery, however, gleefully speaks about this story and how nice his $25,000 jacket is. This is the same person but in two totally different states of mind, based upon being active in his disease or in recovery. That difference is amazing to me because I lived a long time like that, and that's how I viewed things pre- and post-gambling.

Along with lying I believe ego and arrogance are the most consistent and obvious character defects that a compulsive gambler lives with. Gambling does such a good job of building your ego up, to some degree making you feel indestructible. It makes you think that you are better than someone else and somehow you feel good about that belief. It really is stinky thinking at its finest; the constant barrage of bullshit that compulsive gambling continuously allows you to believe. I feel so bad at times for having thought that way, and for other compulsive gamblers who are living with the lie today.

Anxiety is another issue that becomes magnified as a compulsive gambler. You are constantly moving money around, some that you have and some that you don't. You are constantly trying to finagle your next gambling excursion. You are always worried about your finances or lack thereof. Your losses compound with time and your anxiety grows and grows. I lived at least two to three decades of my life with an anxiety level that was not necessary if I was not gambling. Think about that. The stress level that I put upon myself at times seemed insurmountable, yet my juggling continued. Why didn't I simply stop abusing myself? Why, why, why? I wish I knew. Sadly, I don't. I was just taken in by the disease and I truly believed that living with and dying with this disease and being active in it was my lot in life. That is such a sad realization.

Dishonesty is another major character flaw that comes along with being a compulsive gambler. It begins with a simple lie, followed by more lies, to eventually all lies, to stealing, to robbing Peter to pay Paul, to doing whatever you think you have to in order to get that fix you need so bad. Whether it's gambling, heroin, alcohol, sex or whatever the addiction, it seems they all play with us similarly. The diseases are progressive in nature. They only get worse over time, never better. This is so important to understand.

So many new GA members come into the program and on their first day, we ask them twenty questions and if they answer yes to at least seven of them, then they are considered a compulsive gambler. My first time in GA I answered yes to thirteen or fourteen out of twenty in 1999. On March 4, 2011, my second time back to GA, I answered yes to twenty out of twenty. Two questions stood out in my mind that I originally answered no to and now were a yes. The first was, "Did I ever steal to finance my gambling?" and the second was, "Did I ever consider self-destruction because of my gambling?" In 1999, when I read those two questions and answered no to both, I thought someone had to really be sick to ever steal to gamble or to consider taking one's life. I was 110% certain that would never be me, that I would never feel that way. But lo and behold, twelve years later I was answering yes to both of those questions. I truly couldn't believe it was me, that I was in the position I was in at that time. I would say at GA that I would get off by my ability to get out of jam after jam by lying and thinking that it was all right. It was as if I didn't believe it to be lying when I gambled, even though that's exactly what it was. I say this for other problem gamblers, but also for the loved ones who are adversely affected by the problem gambler in their lives. It is the disease within us that causes us to have a view of reality that is inaccurate. We don't want it to be that way, but unfortunately that is how the disease thrives. The only hope for a compulsive gambler and their loved ones is through recovery, and for many that is a fight of life or death. One of my best feelings regarding recovery is that my lying has virtually disappeared or has gotten to a point where I do not recognize it.

Fear is another character defect that affected me when gambling. I was married for twenty-one years yet lived most of those years in fear that my gambling would undo my marriage which is exactly what it did. I also feared being a failure to those I love most, especially my children and then, my grandchildren. I was upset with my ex-wife for some time until I began to recover, and now I no longer feel any anger or anything bad towards her. I know how difficult it had to be to live with me and watch her and I go through the things we did due to my gambling. I blamed first myself and then my disease and am saddened by the fact that I was unable to get to where I am today when I was married to her. But I also look at it that God's plan for me today also included everything that happened to me in the past. We were blessed to have three healthy children and four healthy grandchildren, to this point. We are both in much better and stable relationships, so things really have worked out well for both of us. That's the beauty of recovery. For me, each day forward is truly a day forward, with very few peaks and valleys.

Impatience was another beauty of a defect I had to contend with. All I had to do was work hard, not gamble and I could have been retired by now. But that never seemed good enough. I had to try and cut corners and time with my gambling so I could retire quicker. That's what I would say, but the reality was that the disease had me and was in total control of my actions. Even in recovery impatience is an issue because the days of recovery are so slow; nothing like the crazy atmosphere of gambling. Recovery is slow, boring, and so, so long. That's where turning impatience into patience will really work for the recovering compulsive gambler, so long as they welcome the slow time. By this I mean to learn to rejoice in the fact that no matter how long the day is, the fact is that I was not gambling. I began to relish the slowness. It seemed to me as additional time, time that I was getting back in some way and experiencing in a sober light. Now I wouldn't call myself Mr. Patience, but I am closer to that rather than Mr. Impatience which should have been my title for decades.

Jealousy was probably another factor in my compulsive gambling. Wanting what others had or not being comfortable with what I had as I should have been were also defects in my character. Now I tend to wish the best for everyone and simply focus on me for what I can accomplish. This is such a better feeling to have within me rather than chasing others because I was never happy with myself.

Another character defect for me was remorse, another defect that surely kept me gambling for decades. You would think the remorse would propel you to not gambling ever again, but unfortunately that is not the way a compulsive gambler thinks. Remorse keeps you gambling. Like chasing your money, you are also always chasing the remedy, meaning the remedy for your remorse. You think that remedy is by winning money. But any recovering compulsive gambler will tell you that no matter how big the win, there is not one big enough to get you to quit. It may take you a little longer to give the winnings back and then some, but most assuredly you will do it.

Resentment was another defect that was strong within me when I gambled. I tended to resent everyone and everything if things were not necessarily going my way, and very rarely do things always or even sometimes go your way when you're a compulsive gambler. Such wasted time it is to feel resentment towards anyone or anything. There is nothing positive that I can come up with about feeling resentment towards anyone. Yet when I gambled there was a laundry list filled with resentment towards myself and others.

Selfishness is something you will always hear recovering GA members tell newbies to the program. They will speak to how selfish our actions are and were when we gambled. I can't argue any of that sentiment. When I gambled the last thing I thought of, other than losing, was that I was being selfish in my actions. Yet now I know that my actions were selfish, but I would credit my disease more for that than I would just myself.

Finally, to finish off this incredible list of my character defects I would list worry. It's just what you do. Deep down you know what you are doing is wrong, so you worry about it all. You worry about what if you lose, what if I see someone I know at the OTB or casino. The two last things a compulsive gambler ever wants is to see someone they know at their gambling establishment of choice and to be recognized for being a compulsive gambler. All of this would add to my internal worry from gambling. Here are a few other examples of what I would have to worry about: Am I going to get to the mailbox before my wife? How am I going to cover those checks that I wrote? How am I going to replenish the $400 I lost last night? How am I going to make the $1700 monthly house payment when I only have $1200 available to me? Then lo and behold, the light would flicker on in my head and I would say, "I got it." I will go out and win the additional $500 I need to make the house payment on time and keep peace in the family. So goes the defective mind of a compulsive gambler.

Step Seven states, "Humbly ask God (of our understanding) to remove our shortcomings." Step Eight reads, "Made a list of all persons we had harmed and became willing to make amends to them all." Step Nine reads, "Made direct amends to such people whenever possible, except when to do so would injure them or others." Step Ten states, "Continued to take personal inventory and when we were wrong, promptly admitted it." Step Eleven reads, "Sought through prayer and meditation to improve our conscious contact with God as we understood Him, praying only for the knowledge of His will for us and the power to carry that out." Step Twelve reads, "Having made an effort to practice these principles in all our affairs, we tried to carry this message to other compulsive gamblers."

CHAPTER 13

AL'S EIGHT STEPS TOWARD ACHIEVING A NEW LIFE AND MAINTAINING MY SOBRIETY

My new life consists of working hard, doing the right things, fighting off the sometimes urging of stinky thinking to get back to destroying my life rather than building it. Recovery is a daily event. You must work on it every day. You cannot allow for a day off. Once stinky thinking enters you must fight to remove or reduce it to an acceptable level. All this fighting and reduction is done through your own mind.

I'm personally happier than I have ever been. Being able to live each day without the barrage of worries and stress, along with a single focus to gamble is amazing, certainly something I thought I would never attain. As does anyone's, my day has its ups and downs. It's so easy on a day-to-day basis to get down or allow stinky thinking to influence me. I must work hard at not letting that feeling take over and control my actions. It's like a prelude to the act of destruction. You get down and begin feeling sorry for yourself and your circumstances. Yet there is also another way of looking at things that is more productive and less destructive to you and your life. I mentioned earlier how listening to Joel Osteen on Sirius XM daily helps me to ward off my stinky thinking. His messages of hope, perseverance, and God's love for me always tend to turn my despair into feeling good about myself. It's so critical for a person with an addiction to think positively so that they can beat their disease. I have gone from the likes of prison, insanity, or death to leading a wholesome, productive, God inclusive and thankful way of life. The following are some steps I believe are vital to compulsive gamblers' recovery from this dastardly disease.

Al's Step One – Go to Gamblers Anonymous

For a compulsive gambler to recover, I am convinced they have no other choice at this point in time but to go to Gamblers Anonymous. A lot of GA members will speak to how it's important not to look too far ahead so what I'm going to say may not be recommended by all in GA, but I truly believe that GA is a lifetime commitment for a compulsive gambler. At this point in time, it is my belief there is nothing else available to the compulsive gambler to assist them in reaching a lasting recovery. Gamblers Anonymous does this by getting you to help yourself become and stay clean, and then encourages you to assist others in the program with sharing your story. Every time a new GA member walks in the room, it is my belief you are immediately taken back to your first day in GA. You understand the difficulty that new member had with simply walking into that room. You can visually see the pain on their face. Internally, in the compulsive gambler's mind there is a constant struggle going on. The person knows they have a problem with gambling, but they are also embarrassed based upon the fact of their circumstances and the destruction from gambling they have allowed to occur in their life. You remember where you were in life when you walked in on your first day and it is never pretty. But I think it is necessary for a person in recovery never to forget that feeling, no matter how bad and unhappy it may make the person in recovery.

What I find is that I feel super sad for the new person coming to GA because I know they have astronomical issues in their life, with no hope or understanding on how to correct it. The answer is as easy as just don't gamble today, but the reality for a compulsive gambler to do so is oh so difficult and, in many cases, impossible. So many new compulsive gamblers come in looking for the quick fix and miracle pill. Unfortunately, there is no such thing for this disease. There should be a pill or something to assist compulsive gamblers succeed in their recovery. With technology at the point that it is in our country, very little is heard, if anything, as it relates to treating this disease. I believe going to a psychologist does not work without including going to GA also. Yes, you can openly speak about your troubles, but can you be completely honest and communicate how you think while in your disease? I couldn't, plus I never believed the person I was talking to actually understood how I thought, except understanding that my thought process was messed up. I'm not trying to knock counselors or psychologists as it relates to assisting in stopping the compulsive gambler to quit. They are trying to help, and I commend them for it.

Consider heroin users who overdose. The drug industry comes up with a shot that will reverse an overdose and millions of dollars, mostly American taxpayer dollars, are used to reverse the overdose, yet never actually treat the disease. So instead of coming up with a drug to assist the addicted heroin user to stop using, a drug is created to keep the person from overdosing. In my opinion, we as a society treat the symptoms, but do not resolve the addictions that lead to the overdoses.

In the beginning I went to GA a couple of times a week because the beginning is the most difficult time for a compulsive gambler to avoid relapse. After the first year I went once a week. After year five I go once every two weeks and I do so because I know that's what I need to maintain my sobriety. Many members attend for a couple of months to a couple of years and then they think they are free from the disease. That's not how this disease works. In my experience, when you are in recovery it wants you to think that you have it licked, that you have conquered your disease. It knows that if you fail to actively maintain your GA membership, you will fall back into the old ways of your disease, and it will be game on all over again. For a successful recovery, I believe you must stay an active member in GA and never forget what brought you here in the first place.

Al's Step Two – Slow Down and Jump Off the Crazy Train

Yes, slowing down your thinking and thought process is critical to getting back to living a normal way of life. When you gamble towards destruction there is no way you can do that slowly. Recovery is very slow. When you gamble on a slot machine, blackjack table, or bet on a horse, the activity is very quick. You have a limited amount of time to determine your bet and the activity is very quick. I think that is one of the reasons why recovery from gambling or an addiction is so difficult. It's almost as if you have trained your mind to react swiftly on everything you do. In recovery you must retrain your way of thinking to slow down. Recognizing that not everything in life must be determined within thirty seconds to two minutes is a critical part of recovery.

Slowing down in the beginning is so hard to do. It feels so wrong and unnatural. The urge to gamble is exploding within you and you are trying to recover, telling yourself that you need to slow your thinking down while the disease in your brain is absolutely pounding you with urges to get back on the crazy train again. You need to train your mind to welcome the slowness. Relish the fact that while you are focused on slowing your mind down, you are not destroying yourself and, more importantly, you are not hurting any of your loved ones by taking it slow and not gambling. Those two feelings must be focused on consistently as these are the primary benefits of slowing down your thought process from insane levels where you can recognize the value in not gambling today. When you feel your insides speeding up, go lay out and sunbathe for thirty minutes to an hour. That's what I did my first summer of recovery. I found laying out, feeling the warmth of the sun, and relaxing after work helped me to calm down. It helped me to think and focus on things other than gambling.

Again, one of the biggest things a compulsive gambler new to GA wants to know is what to do to stop. They really do want to stop gambling. They will ask what they should take up to replace the feeling that gambling provides them. Unfortunately for you and them, there is nothing specifically that you can provide to answer them. They, like myself, will have to find their own way and seek out new interests that do not have the same destructive pattern to their life that compulsive gambling provides. Slowing your mind and thought process is a definite necessity towards a confident recovery. I would speak at GA about how important it is to jump off the crazy train of gambling. First though you must recognize it. You must understand that the ride is always the same. It's filled with highs and lows, but mainly lows if you ride long enough.

Al's Step Three - Forgive Yourself and Quit Chasing Your Losses

It took me until my third year of recovery to finally forgive myself for all my misdeeds caused by my gambling. To this day I still don't know if my loved ones, family, and friends have forgiven me, and I don't think that matters. I hope they have but you can't control what you can't control. But I think it was very important to me to honestly get to the point to where I could forgive myself. I can remember one of my favorite people in GA who would constantly tell me that I should forgive myself for what I had done. After my first year of sobriety and throughout my second year, she would tell me to forgive myself. I can remember after year one telling her that I doubt that will ever happen. Then in my second year of recovery I told her maybe someday I could, but I still wasn't at that point. Then in year three, she stopped going to GA and then I finally reached the point to where I could honestly forgive myself. The feeling of forgiving myself for the dastardly deeds I had previously done was like removing 1000 pounds from my chest. It was as if something extremely heavy was missing and because of that, I was able to breathe much easier. I had carried the load of regret in my life for over two decades. I also believe that my gambling disease thrived on my regret, causing me to chase after money lost decades ago with a belief that winning back the lost money would somehow put Humpty Dumpty back together again and make things right. There's no doubt I gambled an additional decade or two by wallowing in my regret, coupled with chasing past losses.

One song that negatively affected me during my gambling and then positively post gambling was the song, "What I've Done by Linkin Park." When I listened to this song when I was gambling compulsively, I would be sad but also convinced that I needed to correct my errors by winning money that I had previously lost and make all things right with my world. Now I'm not a Mensa candidate but I'm also not an idiot, and in my recovery that sounds idiotic to me. But that's what addiction does. It preys on everyone with no prejudice. Whether you're black, white, intelligent, idiotic, happy, sad, fast, or slow, addiction does not discriminate. It is an equal opportunity disease, meaning anyone can get it. The best thing to do is not to begin. That to me is the only sure way of not triggering a potential addiction you could have waiting there within you.

Al's Step Four – Come to Terms with Your Shoulders

I often spoke about the good guy and bad guy within me; God on one shoulder communicating to me and the devil on the other shoulder. I am 100% confident that anyone with an addiction of any kind has this situation, the similarity of good on one shoulder and bad on the other shoulder. You would think that a person such as myself who clearly knows right from wrong would be able to discern between the two. You would think it would be easy to know right from wrong, and which shoulder is communicating to you each time. Yet nothing could be further from the truth for a person with an addiction.

For me as a compulsive gambler, I would swear on a stack of bibles that when the devil would speak to me to do the wrong thing, I truly believed that it was God who was trying to guide me out of the mess I had made with my life. Even before any mess occurred within my life, I have always had this competing force within me. It was always heightened when I gambled though. Now, in recovery, I look back on it and I find it hard to believe how I could have ever believed that doing wrong was the right thing to do. But I do respect the disease within me so the longer my recovery time extends, the easier it is for me to believe my actions when I was active in my disease. You also hear that even though I am over six years into my recovery, I will never be fully recovered or, in proper words, without the disease of compulsive gambling. I'm okay with that. I'm good with it. I'm no longer looking for a quick fix or how I can learn to gamble like so many others can without being addicted. I have what I have. I know what it is, and I respect my disease within me. I will say one of the nicest things about recovery is the fact that it is much easier to recognize which voice is speaking to me now that I no longer gamble.

Al's Step Five – The Strength of Family

I have three children of my own, all grown adults, and four grandchildren at this point in my life. Two of my three kids have children of their own, so they know how important and meaningful that relationship is. There is nothing you would not do to help your kids. My gambling detoured me for a long period of time from being the type of father I wanted to be. That time is lost, and I will never get it back. It's one of my greatest sadnesses caused by gambling. That feeling alone will keep a compulsive gambler gambling for decades, if not forever. But I can tell you from experience that it does not have to be that way. If you allow the disease to keep you on the merry-go-round, additional time would be lost. Money would be lost as well. You would try to borrow from them and anyone who could keep the madness moving forward. But again, it doesn't have to be that way.

You could work the program, pray to God, and stop gambling by not gambling today. You really can do this. If I could do it after forty-four years of gambling, anyone can, and I really mean that. I loved gambling so early in my life that I did not know any other type of life. I didn't know any other way to live, that there is another way to live that does not include gambling. Yes, it's true. I cannot get the time back with my family that I had previously lost due to my gambling, but I could stop losing time with them. I've come to recognize that it simply was that easy. All I had to do was stop and opportunities would occur that would allow me to be included in the lives of my family members.

I do wish that my dad could see me now. I don't think he ever would have believed that I could stop my gambling. I really do miss my parents and my grandmother on my mom's side. I think of them every day, always in a loving way. What I feel best about is that my grandchildren will never see me or know me as the compulsive gambler that I was and am. It may sound strange, but the fact that my disease will never impact them is a huge blessing for me. I love each of them so much and I want nothing but the best for them. They will never know how much I love them, no matter how many times I tell them. The same with my kids. I am so proud of each of them for how they have handled themselves and their own lives while I was out destroying myself for almost a decade. They are all good people and that was my goal. As a fledgling father, the only thing that was important to me was that my children grew up to be good adults. Here's what I mean by good.

I believe there are good and bad people in the world. I have always believed that it was important to add to the good in this world as I have always believed good would always beat bad in the end. I also believe there is so much more good in this world than bad. The only thing is the bulk of those who are good are also quiet. They are not loud or obnoxious. They go to work every day, raise their families, and do the best they can day-to-day while never trying to hurt one another. They are a model of common decency and mutual respect to all, with a touch of common sense added in; all that I was hoping for.

Al's Step Six – A Good Woman

I am a fortunate man. I have been lucky and blessed enough to have had two good women in my life. My first marriage didn't make it to forever as I had hoped, but my ex-wife was and is a good woman; a heart of gold, decent as the day is long. If I didn't gamble, I'm sure we would still be together. Thankfully, in year three of recovery God answered my prayer as I was definitely at a point in my new life to where I was growing, and I was looking for the right woman with whom to continue to grow. I've already lauded Julie earlier in my book, but I cannot minimize the positive impact she has had upon my life. Even more important is how good of a woman she actually is. I will never forget praying to God for her a couple of months before I met her. She is the sweetest woman I have ever met. She is so prim and proper, all of which I tend not to be, but we work. She has the ability to calm me down when I start to go off into my own form of La La Land. I've never had a woman who can get me back on track with my thinking and behavior like Julie can. She always says to me that she continues to learn about me. What she's learning I have no idea, but damn she is so good for me. She is honest and true. My ex-wife always would say to me that she couldn't trust me, and I would never understand why she felt that way and why that was important anyway. Now I get it. I trust Julie and I believe she trusts me. Keeping her trust is so important to me and I think a lot has to do with how I minimized the importance of trust when I was gambling and with my ex-wife. I'm sorry I didn't get the importance of trust back then, but I sincerely do now. Another nice positive of recovery and not gambling is recognizing the truth.

Al's Step Seven – Staying Positive

One of the most difficult things to do in recovery is to stay positive. There are numerous reasons for this to be true; the everyday grind of going to work, financial challenges and challenges that occur to us throughout the day. The effect that gambling had on my life before and continues to have today, even over six years from the date of my last bet, is huge. Instead of being in a high level, white-collar role within a Fortune 500 company, I am delivering sandwiches, soups, salads, and pizza. As a delivery driver you see the best and worst in people. As a driver you are dependent upon people's generosity to tip for your income. Some days are better than others, but I can tell you from personal experience that after multiple deliveries with either no tips or minimal tips under ten percent of the bill, staying positive is a challenge. Even during my lowest moments financially, I have never tipped less than fifteen percent, even for bad service, and typically I tip twenty percent for good service. I am thankful for my job. As a convicted felon, I am thankful to even have a job. I think for a lot of people, given their situations in life staying positive is so critical. If I allowed myself to allow stinky thinking back into my life, no doubt the negative would take over and my recovery would be in jeopardy. I have come too far to knowingly let that happen.

As I stated earlier, I truly enjoy listening to Joel Osteen on Sirius XM for thirty minutes a day to hear his inspiring messages. I recognize that even though my attitude is good, daily I can always use additional support and listening to Joel does that for me. With addiction it's all about the negative. I did this wrong. I'm a bad person. I ruined my life. I'm no good. I can never stop. If I gamble and win that will be my last time. I've hurt my loved ones. All these negative thoughts run through the minds of compulsive gamblers and people with addictions of any kind. I believe my disease knows that is the way to keep me gambling and destroying my life. That is why staying positive, keeping your mind clear of garbage is so important to a successful recovery. You always hear the competing voices in your head. With recovery though, the bad voices are so much lower than when you are active in your disease. Never forget to recognize the good, the positive in your life, even when that can be very challenging. Force yourself to recognize it and then work to remain positive in your thoughts. Never forget this is one of the methods your addiction will use to attack you.

Al's Step Eight – Never Forget

I believe this is critical to my recovery. It's also one of the reasons why I think GA works for someone truly committed to trying to get better. By attending a GA meeting, you consistently have first time members who show up, some at their wits end, but most are simply trying to satisfy a spouse or loved one and to slow down their gambling, but not always to necessarily stop. To stop gambling for a compulsive gambler seems impossible to highly, highly improbable. At some point your hope is that you would get better, learn how to control the disease, and then go back to gambling again, only this time under control like many small-time gamblers can. Unfortunately for a compulsive gambler, I have never seen that thought process play out as planned.

When you start attending GA and the days go by where you are not gambling, your financial situation improves. Based upon the hole you previously dug, getting out of that hole may take longer than you would like, but if you do not gamble in time your hole will be repaired and filled in again. That's one of the reasons so many compulsive gamblers slide back into being active in their disease. Times improve, you are feeling good, feeling confident again, maybe overly cocky in the fact that you have mastered your disease. Right about the time of feeling mastery is the time the disease will club you upside the head, stinky thinking will take over, and you will begin digging another hole even deeper than the last hole you recently plugged up. A lot of this is due to our disease and our character flaws that we must overcome to succeed in fighting the disease within us. Therefore, never forgetting is critical to our recovery.

As a GA member, when a first timer enters the room and begins to speak of their plight, I am always taken back to March 4, 2011; my first time back to GA. I was scared, nervous, incredibly down and depressed with what I had caused myself. Then when you hear the newcomer speak, sweat and act as if all hope is lost, I always remember my feeling of hopelessness as well. As much as I wanted to stop gambling, there was no way I could ever believe that I would stop gambling, as I have never known that to be the case throughout my life. As a member with some recovery time, you feel so bad for the individual in front of you who, at the time, has no idea of the sheer immensity of the disease within him or her. Also, there is no easy or quick solution in recovery. It's one day at a time and when you're in it, they seem like awfully long days. There's also no doubt in my mind that if I didn't attend GA, I would forget what first brought me back to GA. I will not take that chance with my life like I previously did, with little concern for the consequences of gambling.

CHAPTER 14

OLD AL COMPARED TO NEW AL (MY TWO LIVES)

At GA meetings, a lot of times in my conversations I speak about Old Al and New Al. Mind you, I am fully aware that both versions are me. Old Al refers to my life and my compulsive gambling antics of forty-four years. New Al I have referred to as a baby in years one and two of recovery, a toddler from year three through five, and a young boy at six years plus of sobriety. I really do like that analogy of myself and my two lives. Somehow, I like to think of myself as a young boy in recovery who is continuing to learn and grow as each day passes by.

I'm going to start by telling my thoughts and beliefs of Old Al and the life he lived, and then I will do the same with New Al. For me, I find the differences unbelievably striking. Never in my wildest dreams would you or anyone else get me to believe that stopping gambling would cause such internal behavioral changes within me. It's so difficult for me to believe that not gambling could have such a profound impact on me, my mind, and my life. Let's begin because this could take a while, depending upon how deep and true I delve into these two sides of my life.

I have love but greater sadness for Old Al. Old Al had all the hopes in the world but unfortunately, based upon his addiction to gambling, could never realize any or all the hopes and dreams he attempted to achieve. As a young boy, I was always confident and on the cocky side. As with some young boys, too cocky at times. I was a very good student. I went through grammar school with straight A's until eighth grade, when I made a deal with my home room/art teacher that if he would let me read the Chicago Sun Times in class and not do any artwork, so long as I was quiet, he could give me an N grade (Needs Improvement) and I could read the paper. I wish I could have taken a picture of his face as he looked at me quizzically and when he saw I was serious, he agreed to the terms. I finished grammar school with all A's except for one N.

My childhood was interesting growing up on the south side of Chicago, Old Mayor Daley's Bridgeport neighborhood, and a real melting pot of good and potentially bad, but mainly good. I can remember my first year of high school and for the first time in my life, I am doing homework after school, studying day and night, and yet in AP Early World History, all I can earn is a C grade. In AP Algebra the best I can do is a B grade. In Art where I'm really trying as well, I'm getting a D grade. Halfway through the year I come to terms that I'm done doing homework and all this studying. I will do my best while at school and complete whatever homework I can while at school, and my grades would be my grades. Upon making this decision, I maintained a B average throughout high school while working forty hours per week after school for Howard Johnson's on the Illinois Tollway.

Previously I spoke about one of my trips from high school to the racetrack. Throughout my time in both grammar and high school I continued to gamble regularly. I was definitely more progressive in the disease as I grew older, from grammar school to high school. I can remember crying like a baby to get my mom and dad to take me to the racetrack. My parents wanted to go as well, as they were compulsive gamblers also, but as a little kid you don't consider the effect on the finances of your parents this disease causes.

Out of high school I went straight to work in management at the Howard Johnson's DeKalb Oasis in DeKalb, Illinois for Howard Johnson's and my career was off and running. I married at nineteen, had three children and planned on being the best husband and a great father, as nothing was more important to me than my family. I believed I was put on this earth to leave it a better place. I have always felt that way. My way of doing that was to raise three great children to carry on in this world after I'm gone. Now I believe I achieved the three great children who are now three awesome adults. At times, I'm not so sure how I achieved that goal of mine. I know my ex-wife deserves a lot of the credit. She is a great mom and grandmother. I know I played an important role as well, but there will always be a part of me that will always wonder what if. What if I did not have this disease. What if I could have achieved recovery earlier in my life. In looking back, I would have done anything not to hurt and negatively affect my children, yet with my gambling that is exactly what I did. I would have done anything to remain married. Divorce was never in my thought process or any plan of my life. I never would have borrowed money from any of my kids to finance my gambling. I never would have lied to anyone and everyone like I felt I repeatedly needed to over and over again to hide my compulsive gambling.

Can you imagine how difficult it is for someone who believes that they are true and righteous to lie every chance they get, even when telling the truth would leave them with no negative impact? Can you imagine your every thought being focused upon betting a horse or multiple horses, playing a certain slot machine that you know is ready to win, playing your numbers at the roulette wheel, gassing up and playing the daily three and four numbers, along with the Mega Ball numbers? That is the mind of a compulsive gambler. You are totally consumed with the thought process coupled with the act of gambling.

So Old Al was a bad planner. Old Al was unable to set attainable goals. Anyone who truly knows me knows that I am a goal-oriented person, and that I plan accordingly to achieve my desired results. That is the bitch of compulsive gambling. You never know what you have, even when you have it. Think of it this way. In recovery I go to bed with eight dollars in my pocket, I wake up with eight dollars in my pocket. That never occurred when I gambled. One day my wallet would be overflowing and eleven other days, it would be severely underfunded. Even when I made great money and had a great job, my money would fluctuate greatly. Old Al didn't like to borrow but he knew no other way of getting money he needed fast. Old Al didn't mind borrowing, to be honest, because Old Al truthfully believed he was going to win enough money to pay everyone back, no matter how much he borrowed. He truly believed he would pay the money back. Old Al had trouble looking in the mirror as he did not like what he would see.

As a compulsive gambler, you know when you are out of control and that the disease is controlling you, but even with that knowledge you still do very little to change those realities. The disease is so strong within you that you're unable to do anything about it. The amount of stress that a compulsive gambler carries is enormous. You only know the true amount of stress that an addict carries only if you are an addict. There is so much stress. That amount of stress certainly takes a toll on one's life expectancy. The internal serenity of not living such a stressed-out life is such a 180-degree turn from the gambling addict's life.

Old Al also considered himself very weak and weak-minded. Old Al had deep regret for all the bad he had done and harm he may have caused to loved ones or simple passersby. Old Al's ego was a real problem. The progressiveness of the disease grew within me and as it did, so did my ego. But the disease will also take away what it giveth. Near Old Al's end so was his ego. Old Al was a loser. Everything that worried him throughout his life had come true. He had lost. He had lost at life.

This disease breaks you down. It doesn't matter if you are a good person, this disease will beat you into submission. It's almost as if the disease is the puppeteer and you are the puppet. Even more difficult to tolerate is when you have the intelligence to know this to be true, yet you continue to play the role of puppet. Without question, Old Al was a puppet. Old Al did not like being the puppet that he knew he was. Old Al was not a great father. There is no way you can be a great father by taking so much time away from being with your children. There is no way you can be a great father by taking money from your children. There is no way you can be a great father as you implode your life before them in their formative years. Yes, the one thing Old Al truly believed he was put on this Earth for, he was unable to achieve. Old Al did less than he could have in taking care of his parents in their later years. Even though I sent my parents to Las Vegas several times in their life, if it wasn't for my gambling, I could have done so much more for them. For some reason I always thought my parents would live forever. Related to my dad's passing, I could have done so much more for him which could of and should have extended his life. But Old Al couldn't. He was in the midst of obtaining gambling funds, illegally at this point, and he had enough balls in the air. Certainly, too many to catch.

At GA, my first time, they read me twenty questions at the end of the meeting and if I answered yes to seven or more of the questions, I was a compulsive gambler. My first time

I answered yes to fourteen. I answered no to have you ever stolen anything and have you ever contemplated committing suicide due to your gambling. I can remember thinking back then that no matter how bad I am, that would never happen to me. Yet a little over ten years later when I returned to GA the second time, I answered yes to all twenty questions, including the stealing and suicide questions. That clearly shows the progressiveness of this disease.

Old Al could have been a much better husband than he was. My ex-wife struggled for years with my compulsive gambling. I really believe she did all that she could do to save the marriage.

For whatever reason Old Al was unable to go back to GA and admit defeat. GA worked for me for over a year the first time I committed to it. For the life of me, other than being diseased and my disease hitting my pride button, I really don't know why I just didn't go back to GA. Old Al's pride could be misplaced. Old Al's pride could have been influenced by his issues with his ego. Old Al was consistently stressed. Old Al was consistently arriving early to check the mailbox. Old Al was consistently leaving work to make bets. Old Al was not patient. How could you waste so much time and then waste it patiently? That's not how this disease works. When you are destroying your life, each little act towards destruction must be done quickly. Old Al worked a lot of hours. Old Al gambled a lot of hours. Old Al was always calling to check on his horse racing bets that he placed which ran day and night. Old Al knew he could have done better. Old Al thought of himself as a man of integrity, yet deep down he knew he wasn't. Old Al was greedy, very rarely happy with all that he had in his life, always wanting, and straining for more. Old Al was angry. Angry at himself, angry at others, none of which would do anything positive for him. Old Al was able to rationalize anything with his disease to his disease's way of thinking, no matter what it was. Old Al was not humble. When I would win, I would love to gloat and felt like I was on top of the world, until I started losing again when I would feel like an idiot wondering why I couldn't just stop when I was ahead. That is a telling sign of a compulsive gambler because we cannot just walk away when we win. Then our minds gear up and ask what if I won more, double what I currently have and off we go on our way to losing our winnings, along with any other available money that we may have. Old Al was not fully appreciative of all the things he had in his life. He was always struggling for more, not recognizing that his life was going backwards in the process. Old Al was tired, really tired. Life was not what it was supposed to be. How could it be when you gamble?

From day-to-day you never really know what you have because your finances are in a steady flux. You go from winning to losing to winning, to losing again, to losing more, to losing everything that you have at the time. A day or two later you walk out of the casino asking what happened and where did all my money go. That's where reality bites for a compulsive gambler because that's when it hits and you know exactly where your money went, and you go back to hating yourself all over again. That's another difference between Old Al and New Al. Old Al hated himself deep down for all the things he had done to his loved ones, including himself. I truly hated myself. Hate to me is a very strong word, but as a compulsive gambler, it's almost as if it's not strong enough for the way I felt inside. As Old Al I was lost. I was not who I thought I was or who I wanted to be. Old Al was also a bad listener. Old Al was always proficient in speaking, however, not as adept at listening. Old Al was filled with greed. I had so much, yet I wanted more which caused me to lose all that I had. Old Al was not as thankful for all that he had. Old Al did not want to go to GA.

My disease made me feel that I would be perceived as weak for admitting to others that I am a compulsive gambler.

I think people who are not compulsive gamblers consider those with a gambling problem to be lowlifes and deserving of their bad decisions. They do not think or view compulsive gambling as a disease. I can understand why because it took me forty-eight years of my life to admit it as well. People would never view cancer victims in a similar light as a compulsive gambler. The belief would be that we deserved what we received as compulsive gamblers, due to our own negligence and poor decision making. Where I used to believe that as well when I gambled as Old Al, I no longer feel that way. This is a disease. I believe that it's a disease that should have mass funding to wipe out or at least offer some type of treatment. People kill themselves everyday due to this disease, yet that information is nowhere but with the surviving family members to carry that burden for the rest of their lives.

New Al is blessed. New Al has God in his life. New Al knows who he is. New Al is the good man Old Al had always hoped he would be. New Al is thankful for all that he has in life. Being thankful is a huge difference from Old Al to New Al. Old Al was too busy in his disease to be thankful for all that he should have been. New Al is not too busy to be thankful for all that he has. New Al doesn't gamble. New Al knows what he has. When I get home from work now, I count the money in my wallet and when I wake up in the morning, the money in my wallet is the same amount that I counted the night before. Now you may be unimpressed with that fact, but as a compulsive gambler that reality would rarely occur. I would come home from work with a certain amount of money, then go out gambling and then by morning, nothing was ever the same. Sometimes my wallet would have more money in it, however, most of the time there was less money, if any. New Al can look at himself in the mirror and feel good about what he sees looking back. This really used to frustrate and disappoint me as Old Al. After another bad night of losing at gambling, when I arrived home, I would go to the bathroom and look in the mirror at myself and wonder, "Who are you?" Everything that I thought I was as a person, most of it was simply untrue when I could see myself looking back at me. I thought I was full of crap. I don't think that way anymore.

New Al very rarely lies. I'd like to say that New Al never lies, but I'm not 100% sure of that yet. What I can say is that if I do lie, it is very, very rare. The only time I think I would currently lie is if it would negatively impact the person I am lying to for them to hear the truth. It truly amazes me as to how my gambling would make me a habitual liar and would also negatively impact my integrity, my own sense of right and wrong and I clearly understand the difference as New Al. New Al does not run or even walk to the mailbox over ninety percent of the time. Julie traditionally gets the mail. New Al gets little to no mail, as New Al is also no longer saddled with bills and debt. New Al tries to help others now, rather than being totally consumed upon trying to help himself through gambling. New Al is calmer than Old Al. I am no longer solely focusing on how and when I am going to gamble next, and the outcome from those bets.

New Al is prideful but no longer egotistical. In my six plus years of recovery, I have been an overnight stocker and am currently a delivery driver. I'm no longer able or interested in climbing the corporate ladder. I still work hard and take pride in the job I do, but I'm not out to be better anyone else. My work keeps me focused and balanced. I never get too high or too low. When I gambled, I would only get too high or too low. New Al is anti personal loans while Old Al was pro any type of loan he could possibly get his hands on. New Al is cheap or better said "value conscious," whereas Old Al was anything but. My daughter has helped me immensely with becoming value focused when purchasing things. She has taught me many ways to get more from my everyday dollar. This also shows that New Al listens. Old Al liked to talk and to be heard. He had very little focus to listening to what others were saying to him, except if the discussion had something to do with gambling. Old Al spent money haphazardly. Old Al would be cheap spending funds on necessities, so he would have more available money to otherwise use for gambling. New Al is pleased just paying his bills and trying to save what he can.

One of the best things about New Al is that this is the only Al that my grandchildren know. I'm so thankful that my grandchildren only know New Al. There is a definite part of me that wishes that my children only knew the New Al and would never have to reflect on the antics of Old Al and how that negatively impacted them. As much as I like to remove that painful memory for them and me, I also recognize the value of them witnessing the effects of addiction. I want them to do their best never to succumb to an addiction that can ruin their lives. My Dad always said that some of your best learnings are from people you do not want to emulate, as it strengthens who and what you are and want to be and, more importantly, who you do not want to be. That sticks with me to this day. That's one of the problems with addiction. It takes away your hopes and dreams. It takes away you, who you are and who you wanted to be. When you are at such a low level, your disease is happy and content that you are its puppet, and it can do whatever it wants with you. I know that sounds weird, but for an addict the reality is not far off.

New Al is less confrontational. Old Al got off on confrontation. New Al is kinder than Old Al. New Al has more time to focus on others than Old Al had. New Al does a better job of keeping in touch with family members and friends. New Al is more able to help other people with addiction problems; however, the way I help may not be what people expect. I help them by example and counsel.

Over these sober years I have had several friends reach out to me asking for help with money when they have found themselves about to lose their home, spouse, or car.

Sometimes they would lie to me about why they needed the money. Just so you know, Old Al never would have had money available to loan. He would have to go out and get his own loan to provide for those asking for money, and that's what Old Al probably would have done.

New Al is now in control of my life. Even though I know that many times people who borrow would eventually pay me back, I'm just as sure within twelve months from the date repaid, I would be receiving another phone call from them for more money. These people would think since they paid the initial loan back, that I should act as a bank moving forward and provide them with loans whenever they got into a bind. That's how Old Al would think. I could never understand why a friend or loved one would not help when I would have the direst of needs.

Oftentimes New Al wanted to loan some of these people the money. It was an internal struggle with what I knew was the correct thing to do versus what I would have preferred to do. I feel bad for these people because I know exactly what they are going through. Ultimately, New Al discusses his concerns with them about their gambling and not wanting to enable their behavior by becoming a party to it.

Like Old Al's thinking, I am sure these requests by friends seem reasonable to them. They think that if I really cared about them, I would provide the money they requested. They cannot honestly understand why I won't lend the money. Their thoughts are that they would pay it back quickly and how could I be so uncaring and cruel; more evidence of how the stinky thinking of this disease affects the gambler. Such is the distorted life and thought process of an addict.

New Al has integrity. Old Al thought he had integrity, but that was a lie. New Al is not a puppet. Currently my disease does not control my actions or force me into bad decisions. New Al is a great planner. When I plan on doing something, now I actually do it. When I add up the money I will collect over time from working hard, it adds up very close to what I had projected. That never happened for Old Al. New Al is fun. Old Al was a lot of work. Not New Al. He's relatively easy. New Al is so thankful for all that he has. Old Al would never take the time to reflect on what he had. He was always overly focused upon attaining all that he didn't have to appreciate all that he did have. How many people do you think live like that today? If you are counting those struggling with an addiction, I'm sure the percentage is high, although I do believe the percentage would be high on that even for those who do not suffer from an addiction. Why aren't we as a people more thankful for all that we have? Each generation certainly has more than the previous generation. Through the hard work of prior generations, I believe that's why future generations always have more than prior generations. The only reason I'm highlighting this is that I believe you should never lose sight of all that you have in this world, because undoubtedly there is someone who has less.

New Al's ego has lessened. I'm still very prideful, but less egotistical. New Al is less forgiving. That doesn't sound all that great but let me expand on what I mean. Old Al was very forgiving. Deep down I think this was due to Old Al wanting to be forgiven himself for his misdeeds. Back when Old Al was a director of operations for a national company, I managed multiple units and management staff. One day one of my managers decided not to make a deposit from a couple of days prior. The bank called me, I called my manager and at first, he feigned ignorance. Then I called him back telling him the bank had video of him pulling up that night to the outside depository, but it showed him driving off before placing the deposit in the night drop container. I asked him what was really going on and he admitted to me that he was a drug addict and had planned to use the money to buy drugs, but he intended to pay it back. I told him he had until the end of the day to get that deposit to the bank in full, otherwise he would be terminated, and the police would be contacted. Well, he made it to the bank and made the full deposit prior to the end of day. Then I told him to report to work tomorrow and to never do that again. Then I had to convince my vice president to basically keep this admitted thief employee. My boss, the vice president, did not understand at the time why on God's earth I would not simply fire this person. I convinced my VP to give him another chance, but now I understand that decision was more about me than my manager. I really believed that I was influenced by my thinking of when I imploded due to my gambling. My hope was that there would be someone like me who would be willing to give me another chance. So basically, my own misdeeds influenced me to make the wrong decision for my company, my manager and myself. Yet through it all, at the time I believed I was doing the right thing, even though no one else did. I know they thought that way and were puzzled by my decision. So Old Al was more forgiving, primarily due to his need for forgiveness for all he had done.

Another thing that is amazing about addiction is how the disease can turn black and white into gray. New Al views that previous business scenario in black and white. The manager should have been terminated for what he had done. How else was he to learn the error of his ways? Yet it still amazes me that I could clearly see gray when there were only the colors of black and white.

New Al does not measure himself today based upon the sins of his past. Anyone beset with an addiction is driven deeper into their addiction by his or her sins of the past. I know that now, but I didn't when I was in the midst of my disease. New Al is much less angry than Old Al. I don't find myself going off as much as I used to. It's as if a certain semblance of peace now resides in me that was never there before. I am thankful for that peace. I'm more patient and secure than I have ever been. New Al is not greedy. He doesn't have to have everything, just what he earns. New Al is found. I know what I'm doing and why I'm doing it. New Al loves to go to GA. Seeing my friends and making new ones is a blessing. Without a doubt these are some of the best people I have ever met. I want to see all of us succeed, all of us not to gamble, and then to see how our lives turn out. I can say with conviction that our lives will be so much better not gambling today.

Looking at the face of a new member when they walk into the room for the first time always leaves me with a lasting impression. Those times always take me back to March 4, 2011, when I walked into GA alone, scared, and hopeless that there was anything I could do to rid myself of this crippling disease. It's so important for anyone in recovery never to forget the first time they attended a meeting. Reflection is so important in this program, and it always lifts the spirit when you can measure the improvement in your life when you measure from its lowest point. New Al can look at himself in the mirror without disgusting himself. That means a lot to me, as many a night after losing all my money and coming home to use the restroom I would look at myself in the mirror and absolutely hate what I saw. I hated who was looking back at me. All my hopes and dreams in life were nothing like I would experience when I looked at myself in the mirror. How did I get here? How do I continue to gamble? How and why do I continue to destroy myself? My plan at the end was exactly just that. I thought that once I destroyed myself and was caught for what I was doing, that I would stop. Then it would be no more gambling for me. Even though that has worked out to be true, I give myself no credit for executing my plan. The fact is I got lucky. Somehow, I took the slow and steady road. I allowed God into my life to mold me into a better person, while I tried as hard as I could not to gamble today.

What's amazing about these comparisons between Old Al and New Al is the fact that the only thing either one has done differently is to stop gambling. Everything I have written from Old Al to New Al, all of these changes are due to one thing and one thing only, and that's stopping gambling. How can one single issue in one's life cause such a metamorphosis in behavior and understanding. But that's what stopping gambling has done for me. I assume for others after ceasing to be active in an addiction, the results are similar. This doesn't mean that everything is perfect in one's life, but it is so much better than the life I previously led as a compulsive gambler. Yet rarely do you hear or listen to anyone speaking on these radical changes simply by stopping their addiction. I think that is remarkable.

CHAPTER 15

FOR LOVED ONES OF THE COMPULSIVE GAMBLER OR ADDICT

This is as difficult a position to be in as being in the position of a compulsive gambler. I'm sure you as a loved one of someone who has an addiction, or any other type of mental illness, knows the difficulty that consumes your life through the actions of a compulsive gambler/addict. As a compulsive gambler, I believe the best thing you can do is to understand that you can do very little to stop a compulsive gambler from gambling. I believe that is the same for any addict. So many loved ones of an addict get thrown into the roller coaster world of a compulsive gambler/addict and that is not where you want to be. I can tell you for a fact that your loved ones love you very much. Unfortunately, due to their addiction/mental illness it can be very difficult to understand how someone may love you so but hurt you so as well. Compulsive gamblers know they are not only hurting themselves, but also their loved ones. The only road a compulsive gambler can see is the road to where they recover their losses to satisfy the financial aspect of the hurt done to their loved ones. What they miss, however, is that they do not take the lost time with their loved ones into consideration, and no matter how much they win back of their prior losses, there is no doubt they will again lose all they won back, coupled with even greater losses.

One of the most important things you can do to help your addicted loved one is not to assist them in any way financially towards their procuring what it is they're addicted to. For a compulsive gambler, the best thing you can do is to encourage them to attend GA and to keep attending. There is no magic pill for this disease. Attend GA Meetings together if he or she is okay with that. But never, never, never do anything to enable your addicted loved one. For compulsive gamblers that traditionally means paying our bills or loaning us money. You should never believe that if you take care of a compulsive gambler's debt, that you are saving them. The truth is you continue to enslave them to their disease. I know it's hard, and I know the addicted person will say and do anything to get what they want.

One thing I have left out that you probably should start with is to pray to God. Ask other family members to pray for the addicted one as well. Thinking there is anything you can do to fix the situation is simply another form of stinky thinking. Don't do it. Your addicted loved one's only option is to work the program very hard to return to a normal way of thinking and living. So many loved ones enable the compulsive gambler/addict and that is the worse thing you can do. But it is also the most difficult thing not to do. You're a good person. You want to help. You know that your loved one has a serious problem. Yet if you think it through and don't jump on the rollercoaster ride, you know there is nothing you can do to change him or her.

I think the best you can do is to, in a loving manner, provide them with the right options. For a compulsive gambler, that is to recommend attending a GA meeting or to visit with a counselor/psychologist to discuss his or her addiction. So aside from providing the right advice, there is very little else you can do. The reason I say you can't enable your loved one is because that will keep the compulsive gambler gambling. Compulsive gamblers at some point will say anything, then do anything to keep gambling if that is their focus. Their thinking is flawed. It's the exact opposite of what it should be. You probably recognize that to be true, as when you look at them in their behavior you have a hard time recognizing them as your loved one when they can do the bad things they have done.

CHAPTER 16

CONCLUSION

Throughout the remainder of my life on Earth, I hope to assist others in their daily fight with gambling addiction, as well as any other type of addiction. I will remain a member of GA the rest of my life. I will continue to tell my story to anyone interested in listening and in need. One of the things I would like to do differently is to become a voice for the perils of compulsive gambling. There is no such voice and that must change.

You hear on television about new casinos that are on their way; the jobs, the income for the states, but you never hear about how many compulsive gamblers committed suicide over the past year. Somehow, they can quantify two thousand jobs will be created even though nothing has opened yet, but they cannot count the people who have committed suicide on an annual basis due to gambling. This must change. We need to know who is taking their own lives and more importantly, why. There's no doubt in my mind that addiction is the number one cause of suicide in the world today. Why don't we know how many compulsive gamblers killed themselves last year because they could no longer go on with their disease? The same for opioids, alcohol, and any other addictions. All someone would have to do is ask a close family member why their loved one killed themselves and the answer would easily be provided. A loved one of an addict knows better than the addicted person knows what their problem is. It appears all that truly matters is money to the states, federal governments, and certainly the businesses that are legally allowed to prey on those with addictions.

In Michigan you cannot go into a casino and tell them you are a compulsive gambler and ask to be restricted or banned from entering casinos throughout the state. You would physically have to drive to every casino in the state to sign yourself out of each and every casino. They take your picture and have it on file, and you can be arrested upon entering the casino again. I have heard multiple people who have gone back in and lost many more thousands of dollars, yet the only people who were escorted out were the people who would win at the casino. If they won, the winnings would be taken back by the casino and the gambler sent out of the casino. My point is casinos have facial recognition cameras everywhere. If they can catch you when you win, they should also pull you out of there before you lose. Another thing GA has taught me is the extreme number of elderly men and women that the casinos prey upon. They send out mailers offering you free cash to play to visit their casino. What's really sick is that we have had many elderly compulsive gamblers sign themselves out of the casino, only a few weeks later to receive more mailers telling them to come on in for free cash to play the slots. That should be illegal but it's not. It happens every day in Michigan. Why can't you go to one casino in Michigan, ban yourself because you're a compulsive gambler and that casino passes that information along to all the other casinos in the state so that the sick, addicted gambler does not have to step foot into more than one casino. If they really cared, why does a compulsive gambler have to enter a casino at all to notify the casino that they are a compulsive gambler and that they have a problem? The reality of all this makes me sick to my stomach.

The State of Michigan has a 24-hour helpline for compulsive gamblers who are trying to seek help. Try calling it and getting somebody to answer. In my experience, I would need over twenty hands to count finger-by-finger the number of people at GA Meetings whose calls went unanswered. They even play these gut-wrenching commercials on TV to show they care, providing a phone number for calls that will go unanswered. Absolutely terrible. These are a few of the things that need to be addressed in the not-so-distant future to assist the compulsive gambler to get better.

The way I see it, currently the government and legitimate businesses make a lot of money off of people with addictions, especially gambling addictions. In reality, they provide very little funding, if any, to help for those addictions they helped to create. The belief that compulsive gamblers are degenerates must be smashed. This addiction, as well as all the others, affect some of the best people we have. Unfortunately, addiction negatively modifies their behavior, and the pain begins.

My plans consist of letting the world know that by opening casinos everywhere, when we do so within fifty miles from people's homes, a certain percentage of those new gamblers will become compulsive gamblers. I hope to start with my book, followed by a podcast to discuss addiction of all types and to try and help those in need. I would like to speak publicly regarding my story. I think I can help others with addiction.

I want to get even closer to God. I know that will scare many of you reading my book, but I am sure it is a blessing for me to feel the way I do. I could never feel that way when I gambled. I had trouble recognizing the truth that was always in front of me after a night of gambling. I pray to God that I will continue to live my life one day at a time, to continue going to GA meetings, to help other problem gamblers and anyone suffering from an addiction that is negatively impacting their life, never to forget my sins from the past even though I have forgiven myself for them, and to work very hard to die as a compulsive gambler who is not active in my disease.

I'm convinced that most people in this world are good. Addiction removes that goodness, that wholesomeness. Funding for addictions as well as hospitals that are recovery centers are what should be increased rather than building new prisons and purchasing more Narcan. I am not anti-Narcan but using this drug to prevent the overdose deaths of those suffering from drug addictions without providing necessary long-term treatment, you can rest assured eventually will result in prison, insanity, or death for the addict.

www.ingramcontent.com/pod-product-compliance
Lightning Source LLC
LaVergne TN
LVHW090611110826
845146LV00001B/345
9798985654295